To my guardian, E. Perez Romero
For all his labor of love
—Sincere thanks

SARAH'S
JOURNEY OF FAITH

VOLUME 3

SARAH'S
JOURNEY OF FAITH

FROM THE DARK CLOUDS OF CHINA
TO THE BLUE SKIES OF AMERICA

A Thirty-Day Devotional

Sarah Liu

We love hearing from our readers. Please contact us at www.anekopress.com/questions-comments with any questions, comments, or suggestions.

Printed in the United States of America

Aneko Press – *Our Readers Matter*™

www.anekopress.com

Aneko Press, Life Sentence Publishing, and our logos are trademarks of

Life Sentence Publishing, Inc.
203 E. Birch Street
P.O. Box 652
Abbotsford, WI 54405

RELIGION / Devotional

Paperback ISBN: 978-1-62245-470-9

eBook ISBN: 978-1-62245-471-6

10 9 8 7 6 5 4 3 2 1

Available where books are sold

Contents

Foreword

Sarah's devotional trilogy takes you back to a rural, impoverished China and the rise of the Christian faith (Vol. I), through an explosion of the gospel and the high price Sarah paid for spreading that message (Vol. II), and now, to her covert escape from China, to her final destination in a free America to continue to tell her story to the world.

After reading her manuscript of this third volume, I have to admit I was a little embarrassed. Sarah, in my estimation, gives me far too much credit and honor than I deserve. Although her recollection is truthful, there was much more going on by so many others that I feel humbled by her record of my contribution to her story. (By the way, I never received my Wuchang fish!)

Be that as it may, reading her recollection of these events in a devotional format (poignant questions at the end of each day!) caused me to give glory and honor to our Lord Jesus Christ for the opportunity to serve the persecuted in China in such a meaningful way. I could have never done this without the love, faith, and support of my wife, Heidi, and family.

Any of my friends and associates can tell you that my cell phone is a lifeline to the persecuted in China. So often (perhaps too often) during mealtimes, church, and midnight calls, I unhesitatingly excuse myself to answer the phone. Too often, it is desperate and urgent and we have to act immediately to send aid and comfort to so many abused by the Chinese government. Sarah's story, I confess, is not unique, in that it happens a thousand times over.

Persecution in China did not end with Sarah's escape, but Sarah's escape lends another strong voice for the world to hear.

Grace be with you as you read these pages.

– Bob Fu
Founder and President of China Aid Association
Midland, TX
February 2017

Preface

This is the last installment of a devotional trilogy. It has been a real privilege remembering, recounting, and even relishing the work God has done in my life. Then, I'm enabled to share it with you, the reader.

As before, I want to remind you that this is a devotional work and not a theological work. I want to tell my story and that of the persecuted in China.

My recollection of the events may not be exact, but they are my recollections to the best of my knowledge. If, for some reason, you are one of those special people God has brought into my life, and I failed to mention your contribution in these devotionals, I beg your forgiveness. I can say, though, with the confidence the Lord supplies, that you will be richly rewarded for all your efforts. You may even say,

> "When did we see you a stranger and invite you in,
> or needing clothes and clothe you?
> When did we see you sick or in prison and go to visit
> you?" (Matthew 25:38-39)

Jesus never forgets a kindness shown to those who suffer for His name's sake.

My hope is to help answer questions like:

Who am I?

I'm just an ordinary person; what do I have for
Him to use?

Or, we wrongly think He is the God who cares about His kingdom and big things and not about my small and insignificant needs.

When you read this devotional, it is my hope that you will find a fresh and deep appreciation for this great country called the United States of America, my new home, and an even deeper love for the living God whom we serve and with whom we, who believe, hold an eternal citizenship in heaven.

Just as in the closing words of the book of Revelation, that blessed hope we all share. . . .

Come, Lord Jesus.

God is good.

– Sarah Liu

Introduction

My American friends tell me that there is a phrase, "sunshine and blue skies," which describes the happy, carefree state of one's life. I guess that to some degree my use of "blue skies" is similar.

In my writings, I have described my parents as my blue sky, by which I mean simply that my parents enabled me to live a happy, carefree life. Yet it means much more than that. To say my parents are my blue sky is to say they are my everything! They are my world and my life. When I came to know Christ in His love and suffering for me, He became The Blue Sky! As a child, my parents were everything. As an adult, Jesus became my everything.

I have found that Christ permits us to have blue skies in other arenas, although not at all meaning The Blue Skies as only He can be.

America has become blue skies for me in contrast to the dark clouds of a religiously oppressive China. When I became a U.S. citizen I was required to forsake my national loyalty to China, a requirement which I gladly chose, and embrace and love the USA.

Enveloped in these pages is my story, the story of a great and wonderful God in Christ Jesus, and the story of a nation that flung its doors open and took me in as one of theirs. By the grace of God, the USA became blue skies for me.

– Sarah Liu

PART 1

OUT OF HARM'S WAY

DAY 1

Peace in the Midst of Change

*In peace I will lie down and sleep, for you alone,
LORD, make me dwell in safety.* (Psalm 4:8)

———————————

We drove for another half hour. Finally, we stopped. The engine turned off, the doors opened, and the blankets were removed . . . I am free! Surprise mingled with disbelief. We made it.

I rested now in the safety of this new country. No longer undercover (literally), but sitting up on a seat with the dignity of the other passengers. The beauty of the tropical forest, steep mountains, and deep canyon roads surrounded me. The sun set, making the late-night drive exceedingly treacherous over roads that were really no more than roughly cleared paths. Our vehicle slipped and slid, the way so bumpy that at times it became nearly impossible to navigate. Sometimes we got stuck and had to get out and push. At other times we just spun our wheels in the deep mud. Add to all of this the fact that my companions didn't speak Chinese, which left me mostly in the dark about their conversation.

After the tension of our all-night struggle, dawn brought much-appreciated daylight. We reached a flat, open valley.

Here, in the excitement of the moment, we paused to take survival pictures.

By late afternoon, we stopped for a meal at a humble roadside eating stand. My friends climbed out of the car and ordered our food. They returned with our meal, and we ate in the car. Not only was their language different – but so was their food. We ate a type of finger food, easy to eat and tasty. And in all these new experiences, my heart was at peace. I had nothing but gratitude to God and for my faithful companions.

We arrived at our temporary destination late that night. Exhausted from our journey, we all shuffled into a humble bamboo home and were given thin mattresses. In the dim light, we placed the mattresses on benches, which served as our beds for the night. Once I laid my head down, my body relaxed, and I prayed to the Lord Jesus. I thanked Him for getting me out of harm's way from the Chinese government and for His people who guided me to safety. Again, thank you, Lord!

WHAT DO YOU THINK?

I lay in the dark, wondering about the next steps I should take, but I trusted the Lord. He gave me the peace to take the next step. Where is the Lord Jesus guiding you? And will you take the next step?

TODAY'S REFLECTION

_____

_____

_____

_____

_____

_____

_____

_____

_____

_____

_____

_____

TODAY'S PRAYER

_____

_____

_____

_____

_____

_____

_____

DAY 2

Blessed Is My Host Family

Do not forget to show hospitality to strangers, for by so doing some people have shown hospitality to angels without knowing it. (Hebrews 13:2)

Let me begin by making it clear that I'm not making any claim to being an angel. When I walked into the simple bamboo hut home of my loving, generous host family, I was just a stranger. I awoke the next morning in a narrow room (more the size of a closet) that was barely big enough to fit the cot I slept on. I marveled that the room was made of bamboo. In China, we built homes from brick and mud, but here the entire home was crafted of bamboo.

After dressing in the new winter clothes, which my sisters and brothers in China sent me off with, I headed into the main part of the house. Light streamed into a larger room I took to be the family room. Outside, I found an elderly woman and two small children.

Through hand signs, the elderly woman invited me to sit by the open fire. The children were sent to fetch a chair for me. After trying to communicate through hand signs (remember, I am Chinese and my host family wasn't), I shared some sweets with them that I had brought from China. The children stared at the sweets and my new clothes in amazement, as if I were a wealthy person. What struck me most about my new surroundings was the apparent innocence of the elderly woman and the children. It was as though they were untouched by evil and corruption.

Eight people showed up for a delicious lunch. The food was foreign to me – prepared in ways unlike Chinese meals with different vegetables and meats. When the meal began, I thought, Where are the chopsticks? How do I eat my food? As I watched the others, it became clear they ate with their fingers. When in Rome, do as the Romans do. We all served ourselves and, just like in China, they insisted we take more. What generous hosts. To this day, I pray to God to bless them for the love they showered on me.

The next day we prepared to travel, but before we departed, I was made up to look like a local. My hair, clothes, and scarf were all typical native attire. I was ready to blend in – to travel without calling attention to myself.

As I packed and prepared for our departure to Thailand, it became clear that the gift of Wuchang fish entrusted to me to give to Teacher Fu would not survive the long trip, so I gave it to the pastor who had arranged my stay and travel. I said goodbye to my host family and off I went.

WHAT DO YOU THINK?

In America, we are told, "Don't trust strangers." But what if you are the stranger and everyone around you is a stranger? Can you trust the Lord to guide you and to discern whether the path you're taking is the right direction?

TODAY'S REFLECTION

_____

_____

_____

_____

_____

_____

_____

_____

_____

_____

_____

_____

_____

_____

TODAY'S PRAYER

_____

_____

_____

_____

_____

_____

_____

DAY 3

Crossing Over and Arriving in Thailand

Many are the plans in a person's heart, but it is the LORD's *purpose that prevails.* (Proverbs 19:21)

My Thai sister said, "Sarah, look at this skirt."

"Will you buy it?" I asked.

"Yes, I will buy it for you!"

I looked at the skirt and thought, For me? I said, "It is so different from Chinese style. I don't think it would be pretty on me."

She held it up with a smile. "You will be dressed like a native girl and make our way easier."

I nodded, and she found a blue veil for me. In China, this kind of veil was for very old women. I accepted it a little reluctantly. Whatever it takes, I thought.

After I dressed in my new outfit, the four of us set off for Thailand: myself, the sister sent to accompany me, and two brothers. The change of clothes helped me blend in with the local people, which is what we needed, since I didn't have documentation permitting me to travel through the country.

I prayed, "Lord Jesus, I don't know what will happen to me, but I believe I'm in Your hands. Protect me as only You can."

The Lord answered that prayer, and we made it to the border of Thailand without incident. But on the Laotian side of the Thai border we were ferried across a tumultuous river, giving us some very anxious moments. When we reached the other side, we disembarked and were directed to a Thai border station. Since I was dressed in native attire, I must have appeared as just another day-tripper, but my travel companions insisted I follow them closely and say nothing. The gravity of the moment fell on us. I followed closely with head bowed and staring at the ground as we hurried to the simple, one-man border station to secure our crossing. Nothing was asked of me directly. My companions did all the talking and the next thing I knew, we crossed into Thailand with my heart full of joy. Another step closer to my destination – America.

Once we crossed the border, my travel companions and I were handed off to two other coworkers, a dear sister from Hong Kong and a brother from China. We hurriedly said our good-byes and set off with our new companions who spoke Chinese.

After a long day of travel by car over rough and dusty roads, we finally arrived in the city of Chiang Mai in Northern Thailand. My new companions and my traveling sister discussed the best way to get me to Bangkok, because they needed to get me to immigration officials there so they could issue me a temporary refugee status.

They decided traveling by car would be too dangerous because of the many checkpoints and the fact that I still had no documentation. They thought it best for me to take a flight to Bangkok, but without documentation, it still raised the question, "How will Sarah ever get onboard?" We discussed it among ourselves, and finally, a Korean pastor came up with a plan. "I have an idea. How about we use my wife's passport for Sarah?"

The Chinese brother said, "But your wife's picture is so different from Sarah."

My dear sister from Hong Kong said, "I can do Sarah's makeup and perhaps it will be enough for her to pass." She wasted no time and made me up as a Korean woman with an illness.

With the decision made and my new look, we were off in an instant for the airport. It was determined the Chinese brother should shadow me onboard the flight to Bangkok.

The Korean pastor escorted me to the gate. When we reached the passport checkpoint, the crucial moment arrived. The pastor took me by the hand like a loving, concerned husband, and gave his wife's passport to the agent. "Just one person traveling?" the agent asked.

"Yes. My wife needs go to the hospital in Bangkok," the pastor said. The agent stared at me and studied the passport. He said, "Good luck!" and waved me through. I, in turn, like a loving wife, waved good-bye to my concerned husband, boarded the plane, found my seat, and off we went.

In a hurried moment, I prayed, "Lord, I'm in Your hands. I'm not sure about all of this, but You know what's next, and I trust You."

This was my very first flight – ever. Up, up, up we went, high into the sky. How I marveled at the blue sky turning bluer still.

Upon landing in Bangkok, we were whisked away to a hotel where the next phase of this trip would be revealed to us.

WHAT DO YOU THINK?

On this leg of the trip, I was so much in the dark. I was moved about by others. No matter our plans, His plans prevail. Have your plans ever been thwarted or even canceled? How did you adjust to the changes? Or, better yet, how should you adjust to change?

TODAY'S REFLECTION

_____

_____

_____

_____

_____

_____

_____

_____

_____

_____

_____

_____

_____

_____

TODAY'S PRAYER

_____

_____

_____

_____

_____

_____

DAY 4

The Lion King Did What?

The LORD is my rock, my fortress and my deliverer;
my God is my rock, in whom I take refuge, my
shield and the horn of my salvation, my stronghold.
(Psalm 18:2)

U p to this time, I'd been carried along by others. From
China to a neighboring country, I was escorted by sisters
and brothers. I had no clue what was to happen next. From
this country to Thailand, again I was carried along, except
now there was a language barrier. I thought, I don't know what
my companions are talking about, I don't know where we are
going, I don't know anything at all. I prayed constantly and
journaled my experience. Most of all, I trusted that the Lord
was my rock and deliverer.

When we arrived in Bangkok, I was received by a Filipino
pastor and his lovely family who were missionaries in Thailand.
Again, I didn't understand Thai nor Filipino, but I trusted the
Lord and the path He led me on.

A number of important visitors were sent to help me get
to America. A couple of them were a sister and brother from
China who took on the American names of Jasmine and Joshua.
They were in the same situation as me. Then there was a lawyer

sent from London, Elizabeth Batha, whose task was to get me through any legal obstacles I ran into. And Sister Lily from the Philippines was sent to translate for us. Finally, Michelle from the U.S. was to care for all logistical needs. And this wonderful team was provided through the generosity of China Aid Association.

They were a fabulous team that worked well together. I was brought into contact with others waiting to obtain official refugee status for entry into America, and they warned me that the wait would be long. "We have been here a long time waiting for our applications to be approved," they told me. Some said, "We have been waiting almost three years for our approval." They advised me to find a job, rent an apartment, and get on with my life while I applied for refugee status.

I thought, Three years! I cannot stay in Thailand for three years!

After about two weeks of waiting, I had the opportunity to see the Disney animated movie *The Lion King* on DVD. It began as entertainment but, oddly enough, it ended with the Lord reminding me of who I was. I was encouraged by the message of the lost and displaced cub who was reminded by his father, in dreams, that he was no ordinary jungle animal. He was to be king of the jungle.

Well, I reflected, Have I lost my identity in all this travel and moving around? Will I ever reach my destination or fulfill my purpose? The Lord assured me He was my refuge and fortress, and He would fulfill the purpose of my life. My identity as a daughter of the great King was restored in my heart, and my faith was renewed to continue forward.

Finally, news came that our documents were accepted and notice of approval imminent. Everyone marveled at the speed at which the application process and approval took place.

WHAT DO YOU THINK?

Why is it that *waiting* can work complications into our thinking and spirit life? What can be done to stay on track?

TODAY'S REFLECTION

_____
_____
_____
_____
_____
_____
_____
_____
_____
_____
_____
_____

TODAY'S PRAYER

_____
_____
_____
_____
_____
_____
_____
_____
_____

DAY 5

On Eagle's Wings

But those who hope in the LORD will renew their strength. They will soar on wings like eagles. (Isaiah 40:31)

I'm really confused. I turned to my companions and asked, "How do I get to America from here?"

Little did I know that Liz (lawyer, UK) and Michelle (logistics, U.S.) were already hard at work on my application. It was Lily (Philippines), my translator, who kept me informed as to the progress made by Liz and Michelle. Praise God for loving and skilled sisters. As I said before, I was in the dark about the process and what would transpire next. Ultimately, my hope was in the Lord.

Liz, Michelle, and Lily asked a barrage of questions. I tried to answer them while they recorded my answers for the U.S. embassy in Bangkok. Paperwork was submitted, and we committed the application to the Lord. Now we had to wait. For how long? I didn't know.

I was eventually granted an interview at the U.S. embassy in Bangkok. I must admit that when I entered the room for the interview, it looked more like a courtroom to me than a simple interview station. The setting initially intimidated me, but my interviewer immediately put me at ease. His face showed kindness and his demeanor was friendly.

The questions started with "Is the information on your application true?"

"Yes."

"What was your occupation in China?"

"I was an evangelist."

He pressed me further on this point. "What does an evangelist do in China?"

"I tell people about Jesus."

He shrewdly went on to test my Bible knowledge. "What's your favorite Bible story?"

I promptly replied, "Esther."

"And why?"

"She saved her country, and I love China and want to see my country saved too." This seemed to satisfy all his questions.

Afterwards, others who had undergone the application process told me repeatedly that the waiting period could be very lengthy, maybe up to three years. But I had an inner assurance that all would be fine and I would get to America. Exactly when? No one knew for sure. But in my heart, I felt it wouldn't be long.

Liz, Lily, and Michelle worked feverishly to make my refugee status a reality. Behind the scenes, Teacher Fu lobbied congressmen to come to my aid and worked tirelessly to secure my refugee protection status, in a joint effort with the Honorable Frank Wolf (congressman from Virginia), and U.S. Ambassador-at-Large at the U.S. State Department Office of International Religious Freedom John Hanford.

Through their combined efforts, they succeeded in securing protected status for me with the United Nations High Commissioner for Refugees.

At the time, I knew nothing of all this up-front help or the behind-the-scenes help. It was as though I was along for the ride as a passenger in God's great grace-mobile. To this day, I still am exceedingly thankful for every person's effort in securing my protection.

I trusted the Lord, and He renewed my strength for the journey before me.

WHAT DO YOU THINK?

Can you recall a time when you were a passenger in God's great grace-mobile? Were you just a happy passenger? Or were you a backseat driver trying to tell the Lord where to turn?

TODAY'S REFLECTION

_____
_____
_____
_____
_____
_____
_____
_____
_____
_____

TODAY'S PRAYER

_____
_____
_____
_____
_____
_____

PART 2

COMING TO AMERICA

DAY 6

Life Like a Sparrow

"Look at the birds of the air; they do not sow or reap or store away in barns, and yet your heavenly Father feeds them. Are you not much more valuable than they?" (Matthew 6:26)

_____

Tuesday, January 4

"Liu jie! Liu jie! Come here! Hurry!" Jasmine's tone startled me. Is something wrong? I ran into their room and slowed as I crossed the threshold. A muffled voice emanated from the phone's speaker, but I clearly understood the man's words when he said, "Praise God! Praise God! You're on your way to the U.S. Everything has been arranged!" The message stunned me. I couldn't believe my ears. I wasn't expecting to hear this report for up to three years and had prepared myself to wait patiently, get a job, and settle in for the long road ahead, Now, my heart rejoiced in the good news from Teacher Fu.

"I'm really going to America," I said as the reality of the news began to dawn on me. "Going to America," I repeated softly, with joy in my heart. The mission the Lord had given me – of testifying to the world about the Chinese government's persecution of my sisters and brothers – had just taken an enormous step forward.

Wednesday, January 5

The air teemed with happiness, and excitement filled my heart. Thanks to Teacher Fu and China Aid, I had some money to spend on small items to prepare for the trip, and so we fit in a little last-minute shopping for the trip to America.

That night we were given a farewell party. Simple and delicious foods were prepared and everyone was in high spirits. Joshua and Jasmine, my traveling companions, were overwhelmed with happiness and relief too that they were on their way to America. The three of us celebrated with hearts overflowing with thankfulness to God, Teacher Fu, and China Aid, along with all the other wonderful people working on our behalf to make this dream come true. Everyone was excited and amazed that the travel documents had been processed so quickly. Generally, everyone called it a miracle.

That night, as I lay my head down, my excitement was tempered by a heavy heart for the church family I left behind in China. But I was ready, by the grace of God, to walk through the open door before us.

Thursday, January 6

As I prepared to leave, I thought about the Lord's provision. I left my beloved China with a partial bag of necessary items. Now I owned two suitcases of new items. "The Lord has made me rich! Two suitcases!"

We said our good-byes to my host family and raced to the airport in a taxi. On our arrival, we were met by two Thai officials who hurried us through all the queues. Finally, they escorted us onto the plane. Joshua and Jasmine took their seats, and I sat behind them in the next row. After we had settled in to our assigned seats, our escorts made their way to their seats.

As I sat on that plane, words cannot express the feeling in my heart of being loved, secure, and provided for by my heavenly Father. I was a little sparrow in His loving hands.

WHAT DO YOU THINK?

Have you ever been conscious of the fact that you were being personally cared for by the God of the universe?

TODAY'S REFLECTION

_____
_____
_____
_____
_____
_____
_____
_____
_____
_____
_____
_____
_____
_____

TODAY'S PRAYER

_____
_____
_____
_____
_____
_____
_____
_____
_____
_____

We Are All So Small and I'm Even Smaller (Height 4'11")

*When I consider your heavens, the work of your
fingers, the moon and the stars, which you have
set in place, what is mankind that you are mindful of them, human beings that you care for them?*
(Psalm 8:3-4)

––––––––––

"There's another plane!" I shouted to my childhood
friends as we played in the open fields in my beloved
China. Running through those fields, carefree, we were dreamers.

Another shouted, "There's another one!"

We wondered what it would be like to fly. Where are those
planes going? What's in the plane? Who's flying the plane? Many
questions set our active imaginations soaring as we pretended
to fly through the fields with arms outstretched.

Looking back to my childhood now allows me the privilege
of being able to answer my own questions from back then. "I
am Sarah Liu. I'm going to America. I'm in the plane but I don't
know who is flying it. However, I do know Jesus who holds the
plane in His hand."

Exciting doesn't begin to express how I felt that January

6 evening as I boarded the aircraft. The thrill of takeoff was beyond words and, at the same time, a bit unnerving. Up, up, up we climbed into the sky. Joshua, Jasmine, and I lifted off for our adventure to America. So much power, so much thrust. As the plane hurled through the sky I could only think, God, how great You are in allowing mankind to gain such knowledge.

We finally reached our cruising altitude, and I began to experience something new: airsickness. "Jasmine, are you okay?" I asked, leaning forward. No response. "Jasmine, how do you feel?" Still no answer.

She doesn't look well, I thought from the row behind her. Her husband, Joshua, looked alarmed, and at that moment the airsickness bag came in handy for her – then for me. The adventurous spirit we boarded the plane with quickly disappeared. Turbulence struck, and we all could hardly wait for the plane to land. Wait, did I say *land*? When the plane finally made its descent, I became very anxious. I had never been through anything like this before.

While growing up in China, I became familiar with walking, bicycle riding, and riding a bus, a boat, and a train. But hurling through the sky halfway around the world was nothing like I imagined as a child running through the open fields with my friends.

Somehow, beyond the turbulence and airsickness, I still thanked the Lord for rescuing me from my persecutors and allowing me the privilege to speak the gospel and to testify to the world – that world passing beneath me. *How majestic is your name in all the earth!* (Psalm 8:1).

To this day, I still ask in amazement, "What is Sarah Liu that You are mindful of her?"

WHAT DO YOU THINK?

Why does God value us? In particular, why does He value me or you, that He should care for us?

TODAY'S REFLECTION

_____

_____

_____

_____

_____

_____

_____

_____

_____

_____

_____

_____

_____

TODAY'S PRAYER

_____

_____

_____

_____

_____

_____

_____

_____

_____

DAY 8

Out of the Frying Pan
and Into the Fire

You prepare a table before me in the presence of my enemies. You anoint my head with oil; my cup over-flows. (Psalm 23:5)

Y ou may think this strange, especially in light of the title of this book, but I thought I was headed to a greater persecution than the one I left in China. Bear with me as I explain why.

In China, I was told America was a rich country and that I was being sent there to testify to the U.S. and the world about the persecution in China and to the faithfulness of God. But I was also told that I would face a fiercer persecution in this wealthy nation.

Before I tell you about my arrival in America, I want to remind you of my situation at that point. I didn't speak or understand a word of English. I was a country girl, not a city woman. My education focused on the evils of Japan and our impoverished sister state of Taiwan – our estranged sister nation. Whenever the U.S. was spoken about, it was always negative propaganda. But in the church the U.S. was spoken of in positive supportive terms.

As a result, when I was smuggled out of China my indoctrination had a lingering affect. I was confused. I thought that I might be headed to worse persecution, not relief. Now, filled with mixed emotion, I prepared myself mentally for the worse. I held on to the thought, I will confront my enemies in the power of my God, and offered a trembling prayer. "Lord, give me strength."

Upon arriving in Thailand, and specifically in Bangkok, I met up with my new traveling companions, Joshua and Jasmine – fellow Christians also going to America. As we talked about our immediate future of traveling to America and life in the U.S., they made me realize America wasn't an enemy but our friend. What a radical readjustment my mind and heart went through. Not my enemy? We have a new hope, I thought. What, then, lies ahead?

From the window of the plane, I thought, My God! It's so beautiful down there! But I still didn't know what awaited us in New York's JFK International Airport. As the plane descended, I said, "How big everything is, so many people."

Upon arrival, two very stern-looking gentlemen escorted us away. As we silently followed them, I let others explain what was transpiring, since I understood nothing of the unintelligible foreign language they spoke. One hour later, we resurfaced from the immigration office. With documentation processed and papers in order, we were off to baggage claim for another check-in. Once that was finished, we boarded our next flight. Destination – Dallas, then to Midland, Texas.

What's that? I wondered to myself, but Joshua probably noticed the look of uncertainty on my face and said, "Midland is where Teacher Fu lives."

The reality of being so distant from China set in. No Wuchang fish! I thought of the gift prepared for Teacher Fu by the sisters and brothers of our church – the gift I was forced to leave behind. I didn't feel prepared to meet him without a gift. Until now, he was only a man whose voice was slightly familiar to me, and now I was about to meet this esteemed man. Everyone regarded Teacher Fu (Bob Fu or Fu Xiqiu) as an important figure in our struggle. All I could think was, I will soon be meeting him . . . empty-handed.

How strange it was to really think and be convinced that America was a rich country more brutal in its persecution of Christians than China, only to find out, albeit slowly, that my supposed enemies were in fact my real friends. It was as though God prepared a table before my ~~enemies~~ friends, and to this day, my cup overflows.

WHAT DO YOU THINK?

Have you ever been completely wrong about something or someone and God's grace was needed for you to correct your thinking? Are you open to *change*?

TODAY'S REFLECTION

_____
_____
_____
_____
_____
_____
_____
_____
_____
_____
_____
_____
_____

TODAY'S PRAYER

_____
_____
_____
_____
_____
_____
_____
_____

DAY 9

Where Is Midland, Texas?

The angel of the Lᴏʀᴅ encamps around those who fear him, and he delivers them. (Psalm 34:7)

I was told I would need to prepare myself for a long ocean voyage to America. Travel plans were always vague, and I was always at the mercy of the next person to lead me where I ought to go next.

My one-month journey was by foot, car, train, boat, and plane. I finally arrived in Midland, Texas, in the evening. When we started our descent, it was already dark. I still struggled with airsickness and a severe headache, so I really looked forward to getting off the plane. Finally, we touched down, and after deplaning, Joshua, Jasmine, and I collected our luggage and made our way to the airport lobby, where we were met by a crowd of people – total strangers.

What's going on? I wondered as we encountered this small crowd. Loud voices echoed through the lobby, but I didn't know what they were saying. People cheered, clapped their hands, and shouted out chants of "Welcome to America!" and "Welcome to Midland, Sarah, Joshua, and Jasmine!"

We were warmly greeted by all. Bouquets of beautiful flowers lovingly bestowed upon us were delivered with hugs from everyone. All three of us stood stunned. They received us like champions, as if we had done something great. It was just us – nothing more. But they made us feel special beyond belief.

To help you see things through my eyes, let me digress briefly to share my inner experience at that moment. The full extent of my American English was "My name is Sarah," "Thanks," "Bye," and "Love." Beyond that, I couldn't understand a word.

When I first saw the crowd of people in the lobby, I had no idea they were there to greet us. They were very white, tall, and to my eyes all looked much the same with beautiful hair, large noses, and very different eyes – clearly not Chinese.

So friendly, I thought. Smiles on their faces. Though unfamiliar with the people and language, I could see the love of our Lord Jesus on their faces. When they shouted and chanted, it was an unintelligible sound, but by the tone, I knew it was full of joy and sincerity.

For us? I wondered. All this is surreal. Then, from out of the crowd stepped a man – a Chinese man. He greeted us in our language and by the tone in his voice, I knew this was Teacher Fu. "Ni Men Xin Ku La, Huan Ying Lai Dao Midland," he said. Roughly translated it means "You have suffered for the Lord, now welcome to Midland."

We were stunned by his sudden burst of love and joy, and the honor shown to us humbled us. Shock, love, and tears of joys flowed like a river. That moment caught me up in an outpouring of God's love, a love demonstrated by His people. And like never before, I experienced a unity in the Spirit with complete strangers who loved the same Jesus I loved.

Before me stood this man, Bob Fu, or Teacher Fu as we respectfully referred to him, greeting us with this crowd of supporters. I had heard much about this godly man, and now I stood face to face with him. Words couldn't express the fullness of my heart. It was as though I carried all the gratitude of

31

my house church in China in my heart. And now, as I looked into his face – a face like that of an angel to those of us who suffered in China for Jesus' name – all that gratitude burst forth.

We were escorted by Michelle and Apple, two China Aid workers, to the home of Bob and Heidi Fu. Heidi had just recently given birth to their third child, Melissa. There, Sister Spring prepared a large, sumptuous Chinese dinner for us exhausted travelers. The familiar aromas were welcoming. We have arrived, I thought wearily. Seeing Teacher Fu, along with his wife and family, was an immense comfort and encouragement to us all. My encounter with Teacher Fu felt as though we were met by an angel of God. Unforgettable.

WHAT DO YOU THINK?

Can you recall a time when God used someone in your life as an angel? Perhaps a stranger? Someone whose face shone with the love of God? Today would be a good day to express your gratitude for that angel once again.

TODAY'S REFLECTION

_____

_____

_____

_____

_____

_____

_____

_____

_____

_____

_____

TODAY'S PRAYER

_____

_____

_____

_____

_____

_____

_____

DAY 10

Almost, But Not Quite . . .

*Then I heard every creature in heaven and on earth
and under the earth and on the sea, and all that
is in them, saying: "To him who sits on the throne
and to the Lamb be praise and honor and glory and
power, for ever and ever!"* (Revelation 5:13)

———————

A fter our arrival, Joshua, Jasmine, and I spent a lot of time
catching up on much-needed rest. Visits from many
Chinese and American sisters and brothers dominated our wak-
ing hours. I constantly marveled at the fact that we were all so
very different, yet, without doubt, all members of the one body
of Christ – His glorious church. We all enjoyed sweet fellowship
and felt the presence of the Holy Spirit among us. All of us were
filled with such peace and joy, and this was only from visits to
our apartment, which was owned and kindly made available to
us by Golf Course Road Church of Christ. Sunday was coming
soon, and I anticipated our first gathering with the church family
in Midland with excitement.

Sunday arrived and we were all up early preparing to go to
church for the very first time in America. I can't fully describe
the level of excitement I felt. I wanted to hurry to the church so
I could give thanks to Jesus, worship Him with the family of

God, and tell Him everything on my heart. I envisioned myself among all my new American sisters and brothers. The fact that I couldn't tell them apart, much to my embarrassment, didn't hold back my enthusiasm. I still eagerly looked forward to the moment we would all worship together.

Bob Fu (Teacher Fu) and his family came to drive us to our first Sunday service. We're in a car – driving to church – in broad daylight. What a difference from our gathering in China. There, we walked or bicycled for miles in the night to avoid detection by city officials.

Now, Bob Fu and his family boldly drove up to our spacious home, to find us out front, with coats and Bibles in hand ready to go. As I watched the Fu family drive up to collect us, I remember feeling so proud of them all – for being so dedicated to helping the persecuted and helping me. Thank you, Jesus, for Your faithful servants. Bless their home.

As we climbed into the vehicle, Bob Fu said, "So sorry we're running late." He went on to explain that his son Daniel caused their tardiness.

Daniel cried out, "We're not seeing President Bush!"

Bob Fu calmly answered his son. "We are seeing someone more important than President Bush. We are going to meet with Jesus – the King of Kings and Lord of Lords!" I was taken aback with the wisdom of his answer.

As we made our way through the streets of Midland, the church building finally came into view. "Is this the church?" I gasped. "It's sooo big!" My imagination had failed to capture the scope of what stood before us. It boldly stood out among all the other buildings in the neighborhood. Everyone could see it. How different from my days in China, where all our gathering places were secretive and hidden from sight.

Look at all those cars. We pulled into the entrance and we were met by . . . parking attendants? With yellow vests? For church?

How could this be? As we walked toward the building, we were met by . . . greeters? And everyone could see them. No hiding, no cloak of darkness. I marveled to myself. Everything is in the light of day – under blue skies.

We were handed bulletins by ushers who opened the doors for us as though we were special guests – important people. I felt both special and unworthy to be in the midst of this great congregation. I was so unaccustomed to such an expansive setting that I felt awkward, that is, until the worship began.

Beautiful flower arrangements decorated the platform at the front of the sanctuary, along with many lovely people highlighted with lighting. These men and women sang praises to God. Then the voices of all the people joined in worshipping the same Jesus, filling the church with praise. In my house church, in prison dorms and workhouses, I worshipped silently. Now, to hear so many voices raised in praise, I thought, This is like heaven.

If I had to put this experience into words, how would I describe it? Amazing? Awesome? Overwhelming? All these words fail to describe this euphoric moment. Our God is a glorious God. How blue this sky was in my heart. I wished for my beloved China to be no longer enveloped by dark clouds and to experience the freedom of blue skies. This has been my prayer to this very day.

For the service, Bob Fu translated all the songs and the sermon so we could receive the full impact of worship and in hearing the Word of God. My first impression of this first Sunday in America can't be put into words, but it will be forever burned into my memory. It couldn't be any more radically different from gathering in China. In America, there was no fear of the police, no fear of imminent arrest, no fear of being spied upon, no one needing to stand guard outside. We didn't have to keep our voices low during worship, and there was no uncertainty about where we would lay our heads at night. It was almost like heaven . . . but not quite.

WHAT DO YOU THINK?

Sometimes our familiarity with church and worship robs us of the true glory of the moment. Now imagine what it would be like in my beloved China, or for that matter, any other country where the church is persecuted. The contrast is dramatic. Why not renew your commitment to experience the Lord with all your heart, soul, and mind the next time you gather with your church family?

TODAY'S REFLECTION

_____

_____

_____

_____

_____

_____

_____

_____

_____

_____

TODAY'S PRAYER

_____

_____

_____

_____

_____

_____

_____

PART 3

ADJUSTING TO A NEW LIFE

DAY 11

Incredible Generosity

*Because of your partnership in the gospel from
the first day until now, being confident of this,
that he who began a good work in you will carry
it on to completion until the day of Christ Jesus.*
(Philippians 1:5-6)

(A slight digression to revisit my first night in Midland)

After the big welcome dinner at Bob Fu's house, we were driven a short distance away where we pulled up to an enormous house in a quiet neighborhood. Apple and Michelle said, "This is your new home. A Chinese couple, Timothy and Jennifer, along with their two children, are living here temporarily, but you will be in charge."

I thought, This is way more than enough space for all of us.

As a full-time evangelist in China, I had no permanent home. I was trained to live a simple life. A Bible, a hymnal, a notebook, and a pen. One backpack, two sets of clothes – one in my pack and the other on me. One jacket and one pair of shoes, on my feet. Hygiene items were also simple. No jewelry of any kind. And last of all . . . short hair. Never style conscious. Simple was our way.

As evangelists in China, we were instructed to "expect to eat one hundred different meals and to sleep in one hundred different beds." We had no guarantees of food or shelter – a challenge we all freely accepted. We lived with the constant threat of arrest at any moment. In our minds, we understood that we lived with "one foot in church, the other foot in jail." Our guiding conviction was that God would provide and He was in charge. With that, I was content with my simple life in Jesus.

My first night at Midland, Texas, seemed unimaginable to me. The moment I walked into my bedroom, I thought, Look how big this room is! So cozy, so home-like. "My very own bedroom," I whispered in disbelief. "And with a queen-size bed." All the furnishings were new, including my very own sheets and blankets on the bed. I wondered, Is this permanent? The sisters and brothers in Midland treated me like a princess. I was honored and favored. But I couldn't help but ask, "Who am I that I should be here and have all this?" In China, we shared everything with our coworkers. For the past fifteen years, I had been thoroughly accustomed to my simple evangelist lifestyle. But tonight, my small frame was swallowed up by the enormous queen-size bed in this spacious room. The pink lampshade made the whole room so cozy, and I basked in the warmth of God's love and in the generosity of my new church family.

These dear American sisters and brothers selflessly partnered with me, Joshua, Jasmine, and all that we represented. That night I slept with a full heart and a contented spirit.

I don't know how long I slept, but when I woke up, sunlight shined through the window. I walked into the living room, and there I met my host family, Timothy and Jennifer, and their two children.

Timothy worked for Bob Fu and China Aid. He left for work and Jennifer prepared breakfast – eggs, sausage, and toast – a very generous serving, which I came to learn is "Texas style."

I peered out through the living room window. It was winter outdoors, but inside it felt like spring, and the warmth of summer filled my heart. I was really in America.

WHAT DO YOU THINK?

Has anyone ever invested in your life? Your parents, friends, strangers? Now would be a good time to express once again your gratitude for their *good work* in your life.

TODAY'S REFLECTION

_____
_____
_____
_____
_____
_____
_____
_____
_____
_____
_____

TODAY'S PRAYER

_____
_____
_____
_____
_____
_____

DAY 12

Settling In

*"Consider how the wildflowers grow. They do not
labor or spin. Yet I tell you, not even Solomon
in all his splendor was dressed like one of these."*
(Luke 12:27)

"I am the most undeserving person," I protested to God
and myself. "I am the last person in the world to deserve
this overwhelming kindness." This prayer constantly weighed
on my heart and mind. All the love and generosity shown to
us was far, far beyond my imagination.

During our first week, Uncle Doug and Auntie Angie took
us shopping to take care of all our immediate needs. I gave them
the titles *Uncle* and *Auntie* not because of blood relations, but
because of the closeness I felt to them. It was our Chinese custom to bestow these endearing titles on those with whom we
had close relationships. Uncle Doug and Auntie Angie were two
such people. The love of God was made manifest through them,
and we were humbled by their genuine care and concern for us.

They escorted us to the doctor's clinic for our very first physical exam. Then they chauffeured us to register in English as a
Second Language (ESL) courses. I love learning, I said to myself.

God knows my heart's desire. How wonderful is He. From this point on, they took turns providing transportation for us.

Now add to their kindness and patience, courage. Uncle Doug and Sister Jean became our driving instructors. Uncle Doug gave me lessons in his big American truck. He stood more than six feet tall and probably weighed more than two hundred pounds. I'm four foot eleven. You can imagine all the adjustments I had to make to the seat and mirrors to get his truck ready to drive. It was truly comical.

Sister Barb and another sister took turns being my mail reader and American-English tutors. Oddly enough, we started receiving mail almost immediately from some of the most unthinkable places – like credit card companies, local stores, and other stores with the latest ads. My beloved tutors patiently explained to us what all these pieces of literature meant, even the ones addressed to "Resident."

Heidi Fu, Bob Fu's wife, along with baby Melissa, drove me *twice* to the DMV to take my written exam, but I didn't pass either time. Exams were in English only so I had to have help translating the driver's booklet. I was told, "The third time is a charm." And so it was. Now as to the actual behind-the-wheel driving test, Bob Fu took me for that test, only for me to return home without a license. Then Joshua, Jasmine's husband, took me the second time. This time, I came home as a conqueror – or should I say as a licensed driver.

A beautiful couple from Taiwan generously donated their Honda car for my exclusive use. Their kindness was punctuated with deep respect for me. They often said, "Thank you for the opportunity to serve Jesus." Everyone demonstrated such incredible generosity. It was all free, and all I could think was, O Lord, I am the least-deserving one.

After a generous ten-month stay at the church-owned home on Golf Course Street, the church demolished the home and expanded their parking lot to make room for more members to attend. (Thank God for growth.) So, Uncle Doug and Auntie Angie found a new apartment for me, and the church committed itself to take care of my monthly rent.

They brought me to the new apartment and said, "Here's your new place."

Dear God, this is for me? I asked. It offered two spacious bedrooms, two bathrooms, a living room, and a kitchen. Very clean and very safe. What a dramatic contrast to my prison cell with its overcrowded conditions and the struggle for space and privacy. And not one but two bathrooms. If only my cellmates could see me now. Several thoughts like this raced through my mind as I surveyed my new living arrangements. And all this for me. Look what the Lord has done.

Solomon, eat your heart out.

WHAT DO YOU THINK?

The sharp contrast between my life as a prisoner for Christ in China and the love lavished on me through His church is so amazing. Can you recall those types of contrasts in your own journey with the Lord? Beyond words, beyond imagination.

TODAY'S REFLECTION

_____

_____

_____

_____

_____

_____

_____

_____

_____

_____

_____

_____

TODAY'S PRAYER

_____

_____

_____

_____

_____

_____

_____

DAY 13

Clouds in My Blue Sky

"You do not want to leave too, do you?" Jesus asked the Twelve. Simon Peter answered him, "Lord, to whom shall we go? You have the words of eternal life." (John 6:67-68)

———————

I can't believe I'm really here! I constantly said this in my heart as I adjusted to my new country. Every day brought new experiences into my life, and I marveled at the beauty and wonder of my new American life. As weeks passed and life became familiar, I still experienced episodes of new experiences, but they were fewer. The mundane settled in. Clouds encroached into the purview of my blue skies.

Days turned into weeks, and weeks turned into months. A new reality dawned on me, one that began to spread seeds of despair. I asked the Lord, "Why am I here? What am I to do?"

When I preached in the gospel field in China, I was involved in kingdom activity. When in prison, my purpose was made clearer and my resolve stronger. Now, I looked at myself and wondered, What's going on? "Lord, what is my purpose? How do I serve You?" I cried out to Him. "Clouds, O Lord, surround me. Only You can save me from this moment."

At this point, I need to interject that my American sisters

and brothers were, and continue to be, an enormous strength and blessing. My questioning moment wasn't related to them in any way. It was me. I started to feel lost in this incredibly wonderful country even amid such a loving church family. I found myself longing for my beloved China. When you read this, please don't read it as ingratitude in my heart – it was just a temporary lostness, not of salvation, but of purpose.

I asked the Lord, "Will I ever return to my beloved China and, in particular, my church and gospel field?" Again, silence.

One day when I was still in Thailand and Bob Fu was trying to coordinate with U.S. officials to approve refugee visas for Joshua, Jasmine, and me to enter the U.S., he related a story to me. He told me that one day as he traveled from his home to his office, he was very preoccupied with the day's work ahead of him. In his mind, he multitasked as he sped along and organized his day. First this, then this. Suddenly, flashing lights in his rearview mirror pulled him from his reverie as the officer behind him signaled him to pull over and stop. He reacted like one startled out of a dream. He did exactly what the officer commanded. As the officer approached the car, he prepared his defense.

"Do you know why I stopped you?" the officer asked.

"Yes, but let me explain," he humbly pleaded. He explained to the officer that he was in the process of rescuing three Chinese Christians. He produced an official letter from the Congress of the United States House of Representatives, signed by the Honorable Frank Wolf, co-chair of the Congressional Human Rights Caucus, which explained Wolf's concern for me and my companions who were in "imminent danger" from the Chinese government, and that time was of the essence to get their U.S. visas approved.

The officer listened intently and patiently and said, "Oh, you have an emergency situation on your hands." Bob Fu was allowed to leave and attend to his business. As he drove away to continue the rescue effort, he said, "May God bless that officer, for his understanding heart and his mercy on me."

So many questions ran through my mind as I listened intently to his story. How much he loves the persecuted, I marveled. It began to dawn on me that Bob Fu was engaged in the important work of aiding the persecuted and rescuing Christians like Joshua, Jasmine, and me from the jaws of the dragon, the Chinese government.

Bob Fu and his beautiful family sacrificed all, to do the work God called them to do. This meant they might never return to their beloved China. What an incredibly high price to pay, I thought. Then I remembered the words of Peter: *You have the words of eternal life* (John 6:68). I was, and still am, overwhelmed by Jesus' great salvation and the call to follow Him, come what may – even a temporary loss of purpose. He is my Blue Sky. Clouds may come and go, but He remains my Blue Sky.

WHAT DO YOU THINK?

Have you ever experienced a temporary loss of purpose or meaning? Such episodes seem to me inevitable, but isn't it a great comfort to know that Jesus has the words of eternal life?

TODAY'S REFLECTION

_____

_____

_____

_____

_____

_____

_____

_____

_____

_____

_____

_____

TODAY'S PRAYER

_____

_____

_____

_____

_____

_____

_____

_____

DAY 14

In the Grip of Trouble and Anguish

*Turn to me and be gracious to me, for I am lonely
and afflicted. The troubles of my heart have multi-
plied; free me from my anguish.* (Psalm 25:16-17)

How can anyone be so sad with so much blue sky?
Unexpectedly, powerful pangs of loneliness came over
me. Profound mixed emotions uncontrollably swirled within
me, and I found myself being swept away by them. On the one
hand, I genuinely enjoyed the peace and safety of my new surroundings – no fear of arrest and brutality. On the other hand,
I sensed a deep loneliness for my familiar China, my church
family, and my gospel field.

Are my sisters and brothers in my house church safe? I wondered. What is happening to them now? Will I ever see them again?
In my mind's eye, I recalled their faces and memories of serving
Christ together. Most of all, I remembered the voices raised in
songs of worship resonating in the homes where we gathered.

Bob Fu allowed me to travel with Pastor Wang whose ministry was based in Hong Kong. We were on a preaching and
fundraising mission.

As a side note, I have always marveled at Bob Fu's generous

spirit. Even though he did most of the work in rescuing us, he freely allowed us to serve with other ministries. Neither he nor China Aid used us for fundraising events. Never were we paraded before others to inspire giving for the cause. But Bob Fu encouraged us to help other legitimate ministries that needed financial help. To this day, Bob Fu remains a model of generosity and openhandedness. I am honored to be associated with Bob Fu, Heidi, their kids, and China Aid.

During this time of ministry travel, I received news from back home about my house church through Bob Fu.

"At 9:30 a.m. on August 2, 2005, while two American tourists were preparing to have Christian fellowship with 41 Chinese House church pastors and believers . . . in Zaoyang City, Hubei Province, approximately 30 Chinese plain-clothed police officers rushed into the house. . . . The same day, the 41 Chinese pastors and believers from the evangelical South China Church were taken to No. 2 Zaoyang Prison."[1]

Upon hearing this disturbing news, my longing for my church family changed to grief, guilt, and helplessness. Grief is understandable when you hear of arrests, interrogations, and brutality. A deep sadness settled in. I look back on this now and see it was a tremendous spiritual battle being waged against my heart and mind.

Now compound my grief with a stinging sense of guilt. I should have been there, I thought. Then I beat myself with, Here I am enjoying the pleasure and safety of America. Looking back on this with hindsight, I see how unreasonable my guilt was, but at that moment it felt like an all-out spiritual assault.

Now add to all that – hopelessness. I was spiraling downward quickly. It felt like an emotional free fall, that is, until my broken

---

1   Entire article can be accessed at *www.chinaaid.org/2005/08/american-tourists-mistreated-arrested.html.*

heart forced me to my knees for my church family in China. Prayer and fellowship saved me from the grips of despair.

It never ceases to amaze me how one moment in His gracious presence can relieve the troubles of my heart and free me from my anguish.

WHAT DO YOU THINK?

Is spiritual warfare always obvious? Is there a difference between reasonable and disproportional emotional responses to circumstances beyond your control? Do you think one is a genuine concern and the other mere despair?

TODAY'S REFLECTION

_____
_____
_____
_____
_____
_____
_____
_____
_____
_____
_____
_____
_____

TODAY'S PRAYER

_____
_____
_____
_____
_____
_____
_____

DAY 15

I Still Remember . . .

I have not stopped giving thanks for you, remembering you in my prayers. (Ephesians 1:16)

_____

"**R**un! Run! Run faster! They're catching up to us!" I shouted in my nightmare. I woke up gasping for breath and wiped my sweaty forehead with a trembling hand. I often awoke abruptly like this. As my eyes adjusted to the darkness, relief washed over me at that I was actually safe within the borders of America.

I remembered those earlier times in China, and my heart was still there. Yes, there were days of unbearable pain and sadness when I was beaten and abused by police officials – days when I heard my coworkers being beaten and tortured and I felt the pain with them. But beyond this earthly distress, there was also the noblest and highest sense of pure joy knowing that what we did for Him counted for all eternity.

One time my coworker and I were evangelizing in a new gospel field. We were welcomed into the home of a schoolteacher and his family. He told us that he was so happy to have us in his home and that if we ever came back this way his door would always be open to receive us again. Such words of kindness humbled us, and we went on to the next village.

After a couple of weeks, as my coworker and I began back-tracking our journey, we found ourselves caught in a violent midday storm. Torrential rain fell from the sky, and we ran for cover. Soaking wet, tired, and hungry, we realized we were near the teacher's village, so we rushed to his home, remembering his words "my door is always open."

As we approached his humble home and turned the corner, the front door to his home stood open. To our amazement, it was literally open! How odd, I thought, for his door to be open in the middle of a storm. To this day, I still marvel at the *open door*. It was like heaven to us weary evangelists.

Upon entering, we were welcomed with warmth and care. He offered a dry place to stay, a bin of hot water for towel bathing, a hot meal to satisfy our ravenous appetites, and we enjoyed great fellowship.

As I remembered my beloved China, I desperately missed my sisters and brothers and all the wonderful experiences Jesus Christ provided for me and my coworker. But I also remembered those elements I relived in my worst nightmares. Police hunting us down – yet we determined in our hearts to preach all the more. Jail time in miserable conditions – yet we returned to the gospel field to strengthen the church. Even if thrown into Lao Jiao (women's labor camp), we still found open hearts among the prisoners.

Now awake in my American home, the morning sun poured through my window. I pulled back the curtains to see . . . blue sky. Thank you, Jesus. My coworkers are in Your good hands.

WHAT DO YOU THINK?

Who in your life has provided examples of faith and dedication? Why not remember them before the Lord at this moment to live out the words of the apostle Paul, *remembering you in my prayers* (Ephesians 1:16)?

TODAY'S REFLECTION

_____

_____

_____

_____

_____

_____

_____

_____

_____

_____

_____

_____

TODAY'S PRAYER

_____

_____

_____

_____

_____

_____

_____

PART 4

A WITNESS BEFORE THE INSTITUTIONS OF MEN

DAY 16

Bearing Witness before
U.S. Officials

*If you do not oppress the foreigner, the fatherless or
the widow . . . then I will let you live in this place,
in the land I gave your ancestors for ever and ever.*
(Jeremiah 7:6-7)

The Evening of February 9, 2005

732 North Capitol St. NW, Suite A714,
Washington, D.C. 20002

Serious and noble came to mind as I walked into a conference room where I was introduced to the Honorable John Hanford, Ambassador-at-Large, U.S. State Department Office for International Religious Freedom.

I was invited in and asked to take a seat. Bob Fu sat beside me as my translator. Others in the room, to the best of my recollection, were William Inboden, Chris Billing, Rana Siu, Emily Kao (the organizer of our D.C. trip), plus several others.

John Hanford sat directly across from me. What struck me about him immediately was his handsome, righteous appearance. Here is a person with power. He wants to know the wrong that has been committed against the sisters and brothers in my church. He listened intently as I detailed the events of my Christian life in China. Bob Fu was hard at work interpreting and translating back and forth. Never, for a moment, did Mr. Hanford seem disinterested or distracted.

He is really listening to me! I thought. Such an important man, listening to me – a simple Chinese Christian woman. It humbled me to be in a room with such a dignified group. I felt out of my element, but when I shared my story, everyone in the room was deeply moved to tears. Mr. Hanford didn't hide his emotion and compassion for me and for those who still suffered under the oppressive Chinese government.

After more than an hour of informal testimony with questions and answers, I was exhausted. Later, I was told by Rana Siu that she was so overwhelmed by my story about what was happening to Christians in China that she hurried back to her office, shut the door, and cried uncontrollably, feeling the anguish and pain of those who unjustly suffered for their faith. She later told me that our meeting impacted her in three ways, and these were her words:

"First, it was incredibly sad and painful for me to hear about the suffering you endured, and after the meeting I went to my office and cried.

"Second, it really strengthened my faith, and I believe it was close to Easter time and I remember thinking a lot about you [Sarah] at Easter and how you suffered for your faith.

"Third, it was an encouragement in my work because that was a really stressful job and I worked long hours, and often you don't know if you are making a difference."

Moments after Rana entered her office, Will Inboden dropped by and saw her in such distress. He comforted her with a hug. Will and Rana worked tirelessly to help my case, even though they were constantly stonewalled by the Chinese government when they made official inquiries. They persevered, and I was helped tremendously by their efforts. One last note on Will and Rana – what began as a just and righteous cause for the persecuted led to wedding bells for this dynamic couple. The list of those individuals who worked on our behalf is long and noble.

Following this meeting, Bob Fu escorted us to visit with Rep. Frank Wolf at his office (now retired), in the Cannon House Office Building on Thursday morning, February 10.

How absolutely amazing it was to visit with fellow Christians and others sympathetic to the cause of the persecuted. Representative Frank Wolf was no exception. His warmth and genuine concern came through clearly. He freely put his office at the disposal of the persecuted. As far as I'm concerned, he is a champion of the faith and cause. May God continue to bless the Honorable Frank Wolf.

Our next stop was with Rep. Chris Smith, whose office is still located in the Rayburn House Office Building. As you can imagine, February 10, 2005, was an incredibly busy and exhausting day. It was all so very unbelievable but good. Everywhere we went we were treated with great respect and honor. As we told our story to Rep. Chris Smith, he, like Frank Wolf, showed us the greatest consideration.

How strangely odd, I thought, that to the Chinese government we are trash – disposable people, but here I sit, in the office of a member of the U.S. Congress, and he is attentive to my every word. I praise God for men like the Honorable Chris Smith, especially his passion for saving babies from abortion or infanticide. China's one-child policy is monstrous and demonstrates an utter contempt for life. Recently, China has relaxed their one-child policy, not for moral reasons but for pragmatic reasons. It's good Christian men like Representatives Wolfe and Smith, along with faithful non-governmental organizations (NGOs) like Women's Rights Without Frontiers, led by my very good friend Reggie Littlejohn, who are truly guardians of the helpless.

I must mention Judge Kenneth Starr, now the president of Baylor University and an avid defender of the weak and of those of us who have been unjustly treated by the Chinese government. While Judge Starr was the dean of law at Pepperdine University, he brought together students, faculty, and a practicing human rights lawyer from China under the Tom Lantos Human Rights Commission. This generated lectures, testimonies, stories of abuses, brainstorming, discussions, and a renewed commitment to human rights and the Christian faith. Judge Starr was so accessible. I recall standing with friends on an outdoor patio at the law school with refreshments in hand, when out of nowhere Judge Starr came and stood with us as part of the group. He listened and voiced concern for each of us and for the plight of the persecuted.

Later, in September of 2015, just before the visit of Pope Francis to D.C., I met again with Judge Starr and his beautiful wife. His passion and heart for the persecuted hadn't diminished one bit. Amazing! Such an important a man, yet he always has time for the hurting and the persecuted. May the Lord Jesus continue to bless his life. All these noble people have done far more than they think. And I, for one, have been enormously encouraged by their faith and tireless labor for Christ on our behalf.

WHAT DO YOU THINK?

Being an alien. It means to be an outsider to any given community. Which community do you feel alien to? The more I met with these honorable social servants, the more I grew to be a part of their open-armed community. Why not pray, today, for those social servants who make our communities better?

TODAY'S REFLECTION

_____
_____
_____
_____
_____
_____
_____
_____
_____
_____
_____
_____
_____

TODAY'S PRAYER

_____
_____
_____
_____
_____
_____

DAY 17

Bearing Witness before the Media

*The heavens declare the glory of God; the skies pro-
claim the work of his hands. There is no speech or
language where their voice is not heard. Their voice
goes out into all the earth, their words to the ends of
the world.* (Psalm 19:1, 3-4)

I f the heavens can declare His glory without a single word,
how much more can we do so with our words? On this day
in particular, I thought about my words before the media.

Not long after my arrival in Midland, Texas, Bob Fu arranged
a trip to Washington D.C. (see Day 16). There, we held a China
Aid news conference and were given an opportunity to speak
for the persecuted in China. We spoke to media outlets such as
Voice of America, Radio Free Asia, and New Tang Dynasty TV.

I said, "Why did we come here, if not to speak out?" My
mandate was quite clear. I was smuggled out of China and
brought to the U.S. to raise my voice for my sisters and brothers suffering under the brutal government of China. However,
that obligation wasn't shared by others who were smuggled out
of China, which confused and perplexed me.

It surprised me to learn that not everyone was eager to testify
publicly about the brutality of the Chinese government. In fact,

I have come to believe and appreciate that some of my sisters and brothers have a different mandate than me. I was called to go public and raise public awareness; they were called to work feverishly behind the scenes on behalf of the persecuted. Two different philosophies of ministry, one unifying cause. Today, I deeply appreciate those who faithfully serve the persecuted, maintaining a low profile as they advance the cause of justice.

China Aid Association

About a year later, I wrote a series of articles for China Aid,[2] telling the story of the injustice committed against us Christians. We were drowning in an ocean of injustice, perpetrated by the Chinese government, and we thought no one knew about it – that no one heard our cries, except God alone. "How could this be happening to us?" I prayed silently. In my despair, I cried, "Lord, hear your people! Deliver them! Don't let us drown in the cold, dark ocean of injustice!" He heard my cry and the cries of others. He answered our prayers by raising up an association of human rights attorneys. China Aid was instrumental in serving and equipping this incredible organization.

When the Chinese government learned that such an association existed, it used its powers to silence and censor it. To this day, China still tries to eradicate this association with every tool available to the government including harassment, unlawful detention, trumped-up charges, imprisonment, torture, and even death. These brave men continue their legal work

2   (1) Sarah Liu, "For the Love of Righteousness in China," China Aid Association, February 16, 2006, accessed January 2, 2017, *www.chinaaid.org/2006/02/liu-missionary-worker-of-south-china.html*.
(2) Sarah Liu, "Testimony of 24 Christians," China Aid Association, March 15, 2006, accessed January 2, 2017, *www.chinaaid.org/2006/03/testimony-of-24-christians-in-shayang.html*.
(3) Sarah Liu, "For the Joy Set Before Her," China Aid Association, April 12, 2007, accessed January 2, 2017, *www.chinaaid.org/2007/04/xianzhi-liu-for-joy-set-before-her.html*.

under the worst possible conditions. They are truly a light in the midst of darkness.

On one occasion, the association called its members to go on a hunger strike, and I thought the least we could do is join them in fasting. I wrote about them and all the great work they did on behalf of my homeland. As we all fasted, I took to the pen and made their plight known to all who would read the article.

Words can't express the gratitude I have for the hard work of Bob Fu and China Aid. They have once again provided a pathway to express myself in print.

Al Jazeera

The headline read: "China is the world's factory, but does a dark secret lurk behind this apparent success story?" The documentary: *Slavery: A 21st Century Evil*,[3] by Producer/Director Tim Tate.

The e-mail said Al Jazeera. Al Jazeera? I asked, "Who is Al Jazeera?" I was told that Al Jazeera was a Middle Eastern news agency that had a questionable journalistic reputation. "But they want to shed light on the Chinese government for the slave labor we were forced to do. That's a good thing, right?" I asked my close friend.

"Yes, it is a good thing, but we should find out more about the agency and its documentary."

After researching Al Jazeera, I was advised that their audience was incredibly huge and that the project was on the up-and-up. So I wrote back and consented to tell my story – even to a Middle Eastern audience, if need be, to fulfill the mission of getting the word of Christian persecution out.

It was a hot summer's day when the crew of three arrived at the church to begin filming. Tim Tate was the director and

---

3   Sarah Liu (contributing story), Al Jazeera: *Slavery: A 21st Century Evil*. First broadcast in 2011, accessed January 2, 2017, *www.aljazeera.com/programmes/ slaverya21stcenturyevil/2011/10/2011101091153782814.html*.

producer. David Hickman was the documentary host and the cameraman. My pastor stayed with me every step of the way.

"Should I show my face?" I asked with concern. History shows that the Chinese government is very unforgiving when it comes to bad publicity. I also had to consider what would happen if one day I wanted to return to my beloved China to see my father, mother, and family. My mother, in her incredible wisdom, told me not to try to return for her sake. She said she would see me again in God's kingdom. However, my father didn't know Christ, and I was deeply concerned about his standing before our Lord. I asked the producer not to show my face, because one day I hoped to return to China and wanted to safeguard that possibility.

The documentary gave me all the freedom to testify about the brutality of the Chinese prison system and the goodness of the grace of God.

Christian Broadcasting Network (CBN)

I received an email from CBN host Mengfei Li asking if I would come in for an interview for an upcoming video segment. Unlike Al Jazeera, I didn't have any reservations about testifying on the Christian Broadcasting Network.

That Friday afternoon, Mengfei Li and his crew introduced themselves. I silently thanked God. "Thank you, Lord, for another opportunity to speak the gospel."

The segment to be aired was titled *Chinese Millennials Put College on Hold to Seek God in the U.S.*[4] I was thrilled to contribute to the segment and glad to know so many young sisters and brothers wanted to serve Christ with undivided attention.

Mengfei asked me a question that plunged me into deep

---

4   Sarah Liu (contributing story), Christian Broadcasting Network: *Chinese Millennials Put College on Hold to Seek God in the U.S.* Aired May 18, 2016, accessed January 02, 2017, *http://www1.cbn.com/content/ chinese-millennials-put-college-hold-seek-god-us*

thought about my own suffering. He asked, "During your suffering, what was the most painful part for you?" He told me to answer to the best of my recollection.

You've probably had the experience where, in an instant, multiple ideas run through your mind. In this instance, my mind went to the cross. Because of our constant suffering, we tended to gravitate to suffering as a place of comfort and inspiration. Inwardly, I thought, if Jesus suffered on the cross for me, it is a small thing that I should suffer for Him. My conviction was that if He endured the cross and all that happened on Golgotha, He would give me the strength to endure momentary suffering too.

I explained to Mengfei that in a particular instance of torture I felt like giving up and silently prayed, "Lord, take my life. I can't endure this anymore." In that case, God gave me a vision of Jesus on the cross, suffering for me. Enduring all the wrath of man, for me. In my darkest moment, Christ became my noonday sun in all its brilliance for me. I saw perfectly clearly what I was to do. I repented for wanting Jesus without the cross. In torture and in pain, I took up the cross and was taken to the edge of the abyss, and He was there!

Words fail to express that one instance – that one moment in time. Although the segment was about Chinese young people dedicating themselves to the service of God, it was this experience that stood out to me in the interview: Jesus comes with the cross, the gospel is always Jesus and the cross. Jesus without the cross is impossible.

Sundry Other Media Outlets

Several other media outlets were generous in their coverage of my story and the continued religious persecution in China. I'm grateful to outlets like Voice of America, Radio Free Asia, and

New Tang Dynasty TV.[5] Not long after arriving in Los Angeles, I was invited back to Midland, Texas, for a TV interview that aired in 2007.

I am eternally grateful to the several media outlets that shared the value of religious freedom and provided a platform by which I could fulfill my mission in the U.S. That mission was to tell the world what my sisters and brothers have unjustly suffered under the oppressive regime of the Chinese government, and the faithfulness of God to deliver His people. I wanted my voice to be like that of the stars: *Their voice goes out into all the earth, their words to the ends of the world* (Psalm 19:4). The mission continues. . . .

---

5   New Tang Dynasty TV is owned and operated by Falun Gong spiritual movement. Although not Christian, they have taken a keen interest in my story, and my story is centered on Christ.

WHAT DO YOU THINK?

What platforms has Christ given to you so your voice can be heard? What opportunities have been missed or compromised? Whatever your answer – He is faithful to promote godly effort and to forgive our shortcomings.

TODAY'S REFLECTION

_____

_____

_____

_____

_____

_____

_____

_____

_____

_____

_____

_____

TODAY'S PRAYER

_____

_____

_____

_____

_____

_____

_____

DAY 18

Bearing Witness before
the United Nations

For if you remain silent at this time, relief and
deliverance for the Jews will arise from another
place . . . And who knows but that you have come to
royal position for such a time as this? (Esther 4:14)

March 14, 2005: United Nations 61st Session begins.
April 22, 2005: United Nations 61st Session ends.

Preparing in Midland

"We'll protect you," said a very imposing figure of a
man. Others joined in and swore their guardian-
ship and protection of Bob Fu[6] and myself. The meetings, in
general, were a blur to me, but I'll never forget the excitement
in the air. Bob Fu tried his best to keep me in the loop since
the meetings were conducted in American English. In the end,
I didn't know every detail, but I could clearly sense this was
going to be a momentous time for us all.

While I was still in China and in Bible training school, I
learned about John Calvin, a giant in the faith, a significant
man to the world of theology. Now we were headed to the home

6   Bob Fu, *God's Double Agent* (Ada, MI: Baker Books, 2013), 287.

of John Calvin in Geneva, Switzerland, to walk the streets he walked, to stand in the church where he preached and shaped generations of Christians. That prospect amazed me.

Now, I stood at the threshold of this great trip to Europe, where I would testify about the sufferings of my sisters and brothers. I would have the opportunity to tell the world the story of persecution in China, and I would get to tell my own story. God, help me to do Your will.

I'd been told the United Nations was the highest platform on earth to address international concerns, and now I was to travel with a small band of Christians to make our voices heard there – in the highest platform available to man – and I marveled to know that Christ was even above all this. I knew Jesus heard my cries and those of all the persecuted, but now I'd been granted the high privilege of addressing an international audience with the express purpose of testifying about the persecution of Christians.

My friends from China sternly warned me: "Once in America, stay there until you receive citizenship; otherwise, if you leave the country, you may have great difficulty returning. It will be dangerous."

This advice was offered from a pure heart of concern for my welfare, but for me personally, this was another major step in fulfilling my mandate to tell the world about our suffering. So, I determined in my heart that I would go to Geneva, come what may, and testify as I should. *And who knows but that you have come to royal position for such a time as this?* (Esther 4:14) took on a profound meaning for me. Perhaps my moment was not as momentous as Esther's, but it was *my* most momentous moment.

Departure, Saturday, March 26, 2005

All packed and ready to go, we were all prayed up and excited to head to Geneva. Once onboard the jetliner, one of our fellow team members handed me a neck pillow so I could sleep comfortably while in flight. Oddly, though, my first thought was to give this to Bob Fu so he could sleep well.

Once again, my experience shined a light on the differences between western and Chinese culture. We think differently about care. In the west, I've noticed great care shown by men to women. I think they call it chivalry. However, in the east, or in particular, in China, we give great care and respect to leaders and the elderly. Awkwardly, I turned to Bob Fu and gave him the neck pillow to show care and respect for my leader who carried a great burden for all of us.

Arrival in Geneva Switzerland, Sunday, March 27, 2005

After a long flight, we landed in Geneva, Switzerland. I thought, What a beautiful country. So quiet, so clean. Our safe arrival further excited our group as we headed off to a restaurant for a good hot meal. Once we finished eating, some in our group felt reenergized and wanted to tour the city and to take a brief excursion into France. As for me, I was overwhelmed with fatigue and only wanted my pillow. It was important for me to be fresh for the next day's demands.

The next few days we did some touristy activities and prepared for our meetings as invited guests of A Woman's Voice International. And yes, we visited sites where John Calvin ministered. "If only my Bible teachers from China could see what I'm seeing and walk where I have walked," I said.

April 1, 2005

There I was, Sarah Liu, with Bob Fu, speaking at a parallel meeting at the United Nations Commission on Human Rights. The meeting was chaired by Lord Chan of the British House of

Lords. As I stood before Lord Chan, I couldn't help but pray, "God, never in my wildest imagination did I believe that I would stand in this very place, given an audience by such esteemed officials on the world stage." No sooner did I pray this than the profound understanding struck me that I stood before and spoke to the King of Kings every day – a King who loved me beyond measure. The road to this moment had been long and difficult; however, I couldn't help but think about how Jesus made a way for me through His suffering and sacrifice. Because of His sacrifice, I could stand in this privileged place – I could stand before our God because I was accepted in Him.

The conference room filled to capacity. Media attended and I witnessed a sense of astonishment that persecution could still exist in modern-day China, especially in light of recent advancements by the People's Republic of China (PRC). Then, in the very back row, I spotted two Chinese government officials hanging on my every word.

To the best of my recollection, Lord Chan introduced Bob Fu, and Bob Fu, in turn, introduced me. As we stood on the platform, I began with my testimony of persecution in China. Bob Fu worked diligently to translate. After my testimony, they held a question-and-answer time. The nature of the Q&A session revealed that attendees seemed to doubt such conditions could still exist, and on top of that, they held a skewed sentiment that asked, "How could this possibly happen in the twenty-first century?" rather than asking, "How could a civilized China be guilty of this?" The attendees were not skeptical; they were incredulous.

After further questions and answers, the two Chinese officials stood and denounced my testimony, saying in effect, "We have freedom of religion in China and if she was arrested, it was because she broke our law and is a criminal." At this, some attendees and the media turned their attention to these spokesmen of the PRC and started to barrage them with questions. Cameras repositioned to zoom in on these officials. As the cameras turned on them, they quickly exited the conference room without answering any questions. After all that, an awkward silence fell across the conference until the Q&A resumed. This abrupt suspicious behavior of the two Chinese officials made it clear to all present that the PRC was guilty of such human rights violations, and it ushered in an atmosphere favorable to our message.

At that moment, I knew in my heart that I'd fulfilled my mission to "tell the world what's happening to us." Since that time, I've been given regular opportunities to speak in the name of Jesus and tell the message of His love and deliverance.

My friend Stuart Windsor of Christian Solidarity Worldwide, United Kingdom, said, "The vicious persecution of Sarah Liu demonstrates, yet again, the violence used by the Chinese authorities against Christians. Her account is a horrifying testimony of mistreatment at the hands of a regime which seems to use all means necessary to try to stamp out the Christian faith. Her powerful testimony before the UN must spur the international community to do more to uphold basic human rights and religious freedom in China."[7]

April 5, 2005

The China Aid team returned to the U.S. on the day Bob Fu spoke to the General Assembly of Religious Tolerance.[8] Originally, Bob Fu was scheduled to speak earlier in the conference, and we were all to fly back together. Now, because of last-minute changes to

7   Christianity Today, April 2, 2005, accessed January 2, 2017, *www.chinaaid. org/2005/04/chinese-house-church-leaders-to-testify.html.* See also China Aid Association, accessed January 2, 2017, *www.chinaaid.org/2005/04/ chinese-house-church-leaders-to-testify.html.*

8   Bob Fu, China Aid Association, UNCHR Plenary Session CAA Leader Speaks at UNCHR General Assembly on Religious Intolerance, China Officials Mocked for Retaliation with Procedural Tactic, April 5, 2005, accessed January 2, 2017, www.chinaaid.org/2005/04/full-text-of-bob-fu-speech-on-april-5.html.

the UN schedule, we discussed what we should do. Should we depart as planned or stay for Bob's UN speech? Since I didn't speak English, I was out of the discussion loop. It was decided that the team should return to the U.S., and Bob would stay to give his speech. To the best of my understanding, we entrusted him to prayer and Bob Fu was committed to the UN speech.[9] It was there that Bob Fu presented and demonstrated the instrument of torture used by the PRC. This time, the PRC delegation walked out in protest and filed a false complaint against Bob Fu that eventually got him ejected from the premises.

Of course, while we were en route back to Midland, Texas, we had no knowledge of the walkout by the PRC delegation or the unfair removal of Bob Fu from the premises, until Heidi Fu reported what had happened. It disappointed me that the UN kowtowed to the PRC's protest. It was as though the words of Jesus came to pass again: *You blind guides! You strain out a gnat but swallow a camel* (Matthew 23:24).

---

9   See *God's Double Agent*, p. 287.

WHAT DO YOU THINK?

Have you ever experienced a *such a time as this* moment? Perhaps not like what happened in the UN, but a moment you knew God would use you? Why not give thanks to Him for considering you worthy of such noble use?

TODAY'S REFLECTION

_____

_____

_____

_____

_____

_____

_____

_____

_____

_____

_____

_____

TODAY'S PRAYER

_____

_____

_____

_____

_____

_____

_____

PART 5

A WITNESS BEFORE
THE CHURCH

DAY 19

The First Time I Told My Story

Then Peter stood up with the Eleven, raised his voice and addressed the crowd. (Acts 2:14)

Full Gospel Business Men's Fellowship International, Austin, Texas (February 2005)

It was the church and parachurch ministries that opened their doors to me, along with a group of us refugees. I will always be grateful for the first open door to us through Golf Course Road Church of Christ, Midland, Texas, for their generosity in housing us. Not long after getting settled into our new residence, Bob Fu arranged an opportunity for us to share at a Full Gospel Business Men's meeting in Houston.

Before I go any further, I want to offer a quick word about my personal mindset at that time. As an evangelist in China, I had the opportunity to speak the gospel of Jesus Christ daily as we traveled from village to village. Speaking the gospel has always been my passion, and I'd seize every opportunity that presented itself. Wherever a door opened, I'd walk through it.

So often, in our apartment, we entertained friends and guests and shared Christ daily with whoever would drop by. So, when Bob Fu presented this opportunity, I was both excited and eager to share the love of our God. It didn't matter to me who the audience was, or what organization I stood before; it was an opportunity, and I was ready to shout it from the housetops.

Joshua, Jasmine, Timothy (my translator), and I were sent off generously by Bob Fu and China Aid. Bob Fu's generosity really struck me. He sent us to a place where he or China Aid had no assurance of any possible gain except that which is treasured in heaven.

We arrived at a fancy hotel conference room where we enjoyed an elegant meal together. There were probably fifty people in attendance, and after dinner, we were introduced and began the speaking portion of the event. I was introduced along with Timothy, my translator. When I stood up, as I looked out at the audience, what struck me immediately was our physical differences. My features are obviously Asian-Chinese, but when I looked out I didn't see any Asians except for my companions. These are American faces, I thought. The setting was glamorous. Their attire was elegant. The meal was delicious and . . . they looked so different. This entire event seemed a bit surreal. I couldn't imagine it happening in the China I came from. But here I was. I opened my mouth and said, "Thank you for your invitation to share my story." Then I launched out with my testimony.

Timothy, my translator, recalls, "That was the first time I heard a real live story of persecution. As I translated, I translated with tears in my eyes. With every word I translated, it all became so very real – and so intense. 'How could this possibly happen to this young lady?' It was beyond me that this could happen at all. Sarah's story, I thought, was incredibly unique. My life was forever impacted." [10]

Near the end of my testimony, Timothy was so overwhelmed that he could no longer speak, and Casey (his American name) <u>rushed forward</u> to relieve Timothy, and we concluded our

10   Phone interview on Friday, September 16, 2016. Timothy and his wife honored me by being guests at my wedding and reception.

message. Everyone was so deeply moved that it was said, "If you listen to Sarah's testimony, you'd better have a box of tissues with you."

Although the audience was small, God did big things among us that night. What an open door.

WHAT DO YOU THINK?

It seems to me that open doors are rather obvious, but what about the *not so obvious*? Is *trying the doorknob* an act pleasing to the Lord?

TODAY'S REFLECTION

_____
_____
_____
_____
_____
_____
_____
_____
_____
_____

TODAY'S PRAYER

_____
_____
_____
_____
_____

DAY 20

Good Churches, Good Soil

Still other seed fell on good soil. It came up, grew and produced a crop, multiplying thirty, sixty, or even a hundred times. (Mark 4:8)

I prayed, "Lord, You brought me to America, so You have to take care of me, right?" Maybe it isn't a very good prayer, but it was my constant prayer. I had absolutely no knowledge of all the planning involved to get me to America. I simply did the next thing asked of me, because I knew all along that my God was ultimately in charge. I didn't concern myself with planning, nor did I concern myself with any of my tomorrows. I just followed the instructions of the good people God placed in my life.

If you were to ask me, "Where are you staying? How will you survive in America? Where will the money come from?" I'd have no answer. About a week after our arrival, a sister in Christ, Michelle, was going to take us down to the local bank to help Joshua, Jasmine, and me open a checking account. But I had no money. I said to Michelle, "I have nothing to deposit in the bank. I have never had a checking account before, even in China!"

Her response was typical of the generosity I encountered

in the U.S. She said to me, "Now that you're in America, I will deposit one hundred dollars to your new account."

"One hundred dollars!" I exclaimed. I really had my very own American checking account – with my name on it – and one hundred dollars in it.

As I looked back on this awesome journey of faith, with inexpressible gratitude I prayed to Abba Father. I am blessed beyond measure and stand speechless before my heavenly Father.

Golf Course Road Church of Christ, Midland, Texas

I have already expounded a bit on the incredibly loving church family of Golf Course Road Church of Christ in Midland, Texas (see Day 10). I will forever be grateful for their open doors and open hearts to me and my companions.

Mid-Cities Church, Midland, Texas

For our first year, Joshua, Jasmine, and I took online courses, ESL, and worked toward becoming independent. In the second year, Joshua and Jasmine announced they wanted to attend seminary to further their education. They had a clear call to the ministry and wanted to become well equipped. However, my urgent need was to learn English and become self-sufficient. The church family continued to be generous toward us and the U.S. Citizenship and Immigration Services looked in on our progress. So, for my second year, I focused on ESL and traveled with Bob Fu to spread the word about persecution in China.

"Well, Sarah, what do you believe God has called you to do?" Bob Fu asked. "And what resources are needed to make the call a reality?"

I knew the answer, because I'd been praying about it. I said, "I need an American family to receive me, seminary tuition to be reasonable, and some funds for continued support."

Bob's response was clear and simple. "Beginning today, we will pray earnestly for God to make His call abundantly clear."

A few days went by and Bob Fu called me in. He exclaimed, "God answered your prayers! First, we have an American family ready to welcome you for free. Second, we have located a Christian seminary in the Los Angeles area. And third, Mid-Cities Church has committed to support you with four hundred dollars monthly."

I rejoiced. The news was beyond what I could ask or think. I said, "Lord, may You bless Mid-Cities Church for their sacrificial love for You and for me."

"Sarah, pack your bags." Joy shined in Bob's eyes. "You're heading to Los Angeles where a theological seminary is expecting you. Heidi will prepare a farewell dinner for the three of you."

I stood speechless when I heard this good news. I thought, Maybe I should ask more from God! But in the end, I concluded, God is God. Even a thousand requests make no difference to Him.

At the farewell dinner with the Fu family, Joshua and Jasmine listened intently about all that had transpired and my plans for going to Los Angeles for a seminary education. They loved the plan so much that they too decided to go to Los Angeles for seminary training. So we all packed our living essentials and said our good-byes to our Midland friends and church family. Next stop . . . Los Angeles.

It must be said that the Mid-Cities Church faithfully continued to support me financially for two years. Every month, I regularly received $400. That's $4,800 a year, and that's $9,600 for the entire commitment. Such generosity made me feel cared for in the Father's hands. Thank you, Mid-Cities Church, for being His hands.

My prayer was and still is "God, in the past, You revealed Yourself as my mom's almighty God and now, mine too. I will use every penny You put into my hands to glorify You. I will push myself to be a good student and extend the blessing from Mid-Cities Church. I pray that their investment in me produces a crop of some thirty, sixty, and one hundred times over to others."

Pastor Daniel and Mid-Cities Church brothers and sisters, you played an important role in my journey of faith. I am eternally grateful.

WHAT DO YOU THINK?

All of us benefit from being a part of the family of God. God gives us His Spirit, the Scriptures, the saints, and the shepherds. Now would be a great time to give thanks for the church and to renew your effort to share in its mission.

TODAY'S REFLECTION

_____

_____

_____

_____

_____

_____

_____

_____

_____

_____

_____

TODAY'S PRAYER

_____

_____

_____

_____

_____

_____

DAY 21

You Did for Me

The King will reply, "Truly I tell you, whatever you did for one of the least of these brothers and sisters of mine, you did for me." (Matthew 25:40)

Hacienda Christian Fellowship

Upon arriving in Los Angeles, and in particular, La Puente, California, my first big new family was Hacienda Christian Fellowship (HCF). They loved me unconditionally and cared about me without reservation. I didn't need to speak good American English nor did they require me to do service in the church. They just loved me, simply because I was a child of God.

At that moment, reflecting on all that I had gone through in China, I felt like a bird with a broken wing. Here, at this church, I found healing and care like a little bird taking refuge beneath the branches of a tree. Day by day, strength returned. The broken wing healed, and now I could fly into the blue sky . . . again.

As Christmas 2007 approached, life was in full swing. For me, that meant being a full-time seminary student, full-time ESL student, and part-time employee so I could repay dental fees. My days were full and busy, and my purpose renewed, my direction clear. But oh, how exhausting it was. It was a *good* tired, though. Amidst all this, the fact that my stay with the Romeros was room-and-board free reassured me. How grateful I was for another kindness to me.

The question, *Who am I that You are mindful of me?* filled my heart. But He assured me that I was His daughter, loved by Him, cared for by His people.

We finished our Christmas breakfast of tamales and eggs and were about to move the celebration to the living room when Pastor Bob Wilcox slipped to my side and secretly passed an envelope into my hands. He said, "This gift is from HCF and Merry Christmas." I opened it and stared in awe at a three thousand-dollar check. At that moment, gratefulness filled me, but what I valued above all was the sacrificial love from my new church family. Blessing upon blessing. Their love for me was overwhelming. They sacrificed for me, and it was never about what they could get from me. They loved me. It refreshed my spirit. I felt renewed and whole again, enabled to face the long journey of life before me.

Sometime later, I became engaged to be married. A close Chinese friend told me that her wedding was very simple: the groom and bride, and a few friends sharing a meal after the ceremony. In my heart of hearts, I wanted my special day to be more than that, but, of course, how could it be?

Shortly after this conversation, I discussed my humble wedding plans with my guardian, Pastor Eddie. In that brief discussion, he shared so many good ideas, but I secretly thought all of them were beyond my means. My guardian confidently said, "Let's do the wedding and reception in a way that brings glory to our God. Let's do our best."

One week later, a planning team was assembled. Each person served with all their heart (and free of charge) with the clear goal of blessing me and glorifying God. They really meant it. It amazed me to see them all at work to make my big day happen. The planning team was composed of six brothers and sisters. Each played a different role as they worked tirelessly in unison for three months until the big day arrived. Pastor Eddie and Rosie were the overseers, Helen Aguilar was the coordinator, Eddie and Nannette Lugo took charge of design and setup, and Javen Frausto, food preparation. (Boy, can this guy cook!) Lizette Martinez was our baker and Jason Tucker was our videographer and media tech.

Hacienda Christian Fellowship made me feel like a princess. From wedding plans to wedding day, I was shown great love and favor.

Refuge Calvary Chapel, Huntington Beach

The first time I met Pastor Bill Welsh was in the parking lot of Hacienda Christian Fellowship during a rally for Pastor Eddie's China event, "Let My People Go!" in mid-2008. At that time, I didn't even know he was a pastor. He seemed so unpretentious and casual, with no air of formality.

When Pastor Bill invited me to share briefly my testimony at Refuge Calvary Chapel, Huntington Beach, California, we all experienced a holy moment. Pastor Bill and the entire church were so deeply moved. Even now, recalling that day, those precious faith-building moments stir my spirit to a deep love for this church and its wonderful leaders. Following the showing of my brief video, I was presented to the church. As I stepped before them on the platform, they spontaneously stood, filling the sanctuary with applause, shouts, and tears. Pastor Bill, deeply moved, could hardly speak. When he had composed himself, he said, "I had prepared much to say, but after this young lady's testimony, I don't know what I can contribute." All of us on the platform were taken by surprise by this Spirit-filled moment, and we gave thanks and praise to our God and King, Jesus Christ.

The church vowed to support me generously every month. For the next five years, they faithfully contributed to my needs. They *did for me*, and may our God continue to bless them for their sacrifice.

California International Theological Seminary

The generosity of Refuge Calvary Chapel, Huntington Beach, made it possible for me to continue my studies in seminary. In addition, California International Theological Seminary (CITS) sacrificed to make my educational dream a reality. The seminary supported me by underwriting two-thirds of my tuition, thus, *doing for me* a generous thing.

Special thanks to CITS President Dr. Huang Sheng Xian, the faculty, the staff, and my fellowship students. I am deeply grateful.

WHAT DO YOU THINK?

Take a moment and recall those who have *done for you* – done good things that lifted your spirit and helped you flourish. Why not give thanks for them as the Lord reminds you of each of them?

TODAY'S REFLECTION

_____

_____

_____

_____

_____

_____

_____

_____

_____

_____

_____

_____

_____

TODAY'S PRAYER

_____

_____

_____

_____

_____

_____

_____

DAY 22

China Aid Association and Voice of the Martyrs

Speak up for those who cannot speak for themselves,
for the rights of all who are destitute. Speak up and
judge fairly; defend the rights of the poor and needy.
(Proverbs 31:8-9)

China Aid Association

To begin, China Aid Association (CAA) is woven through-out this entire book. The fact that I can write these words on this page, sitting in this place, is due to the fact that God used CAA to make this moment possible.

China Aid was my lifeline to America, plain and simple. I want to say thanks to China Aid, but words utterly fail to capture my deep, heartfelt gratitude for what Bob Fu and all CAA have done for the suffering church in China and for me personally.

The name of Bob Fu and the work of China Aid is known throughout the underground church (house churches) in China. Though they'd never met Bob Fu, my church and all the leaders knew he was our friend, and they trusted him implicitly. Clearly, I could say his reputation preceded him. He earned the love and respect of our church – yet we had never met him.

When our church went through its darkest moments because of the unrelenting state-sponsored persecution, China Aid and Bob Fu were stars shining in a night sky. We all knew we had a friend in Bob Fu and that perhaps God had raised him up for such a time as this. His passion and untiring dedication for speaking out emboldened us in the faith. I think of Bob Fu as a kind of Nehemiah, whose heart broke for his people.

> They said to me, "Those who survived the exile
> and are back in the province are in great trouble
> and disgrace. The wall of Jerusalem is broken
> down, and its gates have been burned with fire."
> When I heard these things, I sat down and wept.
> (Nehemiah 1:3-4a)

We knew he was one of us, both as a Christian and as a Chinese, and that he was familiar with our plight. He and Heidi had endured persecution themselves. Just the mention of China Aid and Bob Fu reminded us that we were neither helpless nor forgotten.

When at our weakest, Bob Fu and China Aid came to our rescue with desperately needed support. My house church leaders connected with Bob Fu and the bond of friendship formed, along with a lifeline to the outside world. American Christians joined in our suffering through China Aid . . . and we knew it. As a result, I was prayerfully selected by my leaders and Bob Fu to escape the dragon's grasp. This act enabled me to tell the outside world what was happening to our church. This I do to this day.

China Aid and Bob Fu, the Lord heard your cry and saw your tears.

Voice of the Martyrs
Through the many kindnesses of Bob Fu, I was introduced to

Voice of the Martyrs (VOM). If China Aid and Bob Fu were a lifeline, VOM became a platform, a stage from which I've spoken the message of God's faithfulness to the persecuted Christians of China – a message of faith and hope in our Lord Jesus Christ.

My very first contact with VOM was a visit from Midland, Texas, to Bartlesville, Oklahoma, with Bob and Heidi Fu and family. My first impression of their work deeply touched me. Here was a work of God dedicated to people like me. As I toured the facility, picture after picture of persecuted sisters and brothers from all over the world hung on their walls and in their hallways. They provided a constant reminder of that part of the church which was in deep trouble and experiencing unbearable hardships.

Though I knew hardly any American English, the pictures told the whole story to me. I turned the corner, and my eyes fell on pictures of my co-workers LiYing, Sheng MingHua, and Pastor Gong. Renewed heartache flooded my eyes with tears. Tears cascaded down my cheeks as I quietly prayed, "God, You have never forsaken us." This moment, in the hallways of VOM, my mind flashed back and forth to China and this hallway. I sensed the Lord's assurance: "I was always there." How I wished I could call all my church family in China and tell them what I witnessed hanging on the walls of VOM. "He is always there!"

I am happy to report that VOM and I have developed a wonderful partnership in the gospel. As a regular guest speaker at VOM conferences, they have given me a platform from which to speak up for the persecuted. Thank you, VOM.

WHAT DO YOU THINK?

Who has God used as your lifeline? Who has given you a place to be heard? Consider this: why not become a lifeline to another or a listening ear to hear their story?

TODAY'S REFLECTION

_____

_____

_____

_____

_____

_____

_____

_____

_____

_____

_____

_____

TODAY'S PRAYER

_____

_____

_____

_____

_____

_____

_____

_____

DAY 23

California, Here I Come

*The law from your mouth is more precious to
me than thousands of pieces of silver and gold.*
(Psalm 119:72)

—————

Just before I moved to California, I applied for a low-income
apartment in Midland. Management told me I'd be put on
a waiting list. "There are eleven applicants ahead of you." They
left me with the impression that this process could take quite
some time.

O Lord, I thought, how will I ever get my new life started?
School, work, church, a future. It all seemed to press in on me,
so I cried out to the Lord again, "Jesus, I desperately need this
apartment." I ended my prayer with "Please, please take care of
me!" He assured my heart that He would take care of me and
that nothing was too hard for Him.

One short week later, while shopping at Walmart, I received
a call from the manager of the apartments. But I didn't understand a word he said; it was all English to me. I wasn't sure
what the manager understood in our exchange, so I wanted
to go to his office with a friend who could translate. When we
arrived, he ushered us in to his office and invited us to sit in
chairs near his desk. Then, with an ear-to-ear grin, he proudly

announced that the apartment was awarded to me and that it would be rent-FREE!

A miracle, Lord! That's what You've done – a miracle! He also reported that I was free to move in that weekend. As you can imagine, I was overwhelmed by His grace and kindness to me, a simple woman in His loving care. Now I had my own place to launch my new life.

Out of wonder, I asked the manager again, "What is the monthly rent?"

He verified the unthinkable as he clearly enunciated, "Zero!" Then, probably to make sure I was absolutely clear on the terms, he raised his hand and touched his thumb and index finger together signifying "0."

Wow! I thought. This is my God, this is America. My friends helped me move in to the apartment that weekend. It was exhausting, yet we all were full of joy. With the work of moving in complete, I sat in my new American apartment, with a heart full of gratitude to my God who gives me everything and uses so many wonderful people to make it happen. I was humbled.

Early one morning, a neighbor came to my door and told me that I needed to report to the manager's office . . . something about a check. It filled me with a bit of concern that perhaps I didn't understand the arrangement properly and now I'd have to go pay something. Armed with my English dictionary and my new checkbook, I made my way to the manager's office. While I waited, I looked up the word "rent." The manager presented me with a check. I leaned over to inspect this check to see if I could recognize any symbols. And there, in the middle of the check was my Chinese name. I didn't understand, so I asked, "What is the meaning of the check?"

He replied that it was provided to pay for heating in my apartment so I could stay warm during these cold Texas nights. In amazement, I doubled checked the meaning of "keep warm" in my dictionary. To keep warm – my God and these wonderful people cared about me keeping warm. Yes, outside it was cold, but now, in my heart, the warmth of kindness filled my soul.

Now my life in Midland was taking off. The college was just down the street, and I found a part-time job. Life was good. *I'm a long way away from Liao Jiao.*

Wait, There's More

Not long afterwards, Bob Fu came to me and announced, "All your prayers have been answered!"

I thought, Of course they have. I'm free in America, I have many friends, a church family, food, a free apartment, and let us not forget a warmth check for the winter.

Bob Fu's eyes shined with excitement. "Seminary school! You've been accepted at seminary school!"

The option of seminary school! This news came much sooner than I expected.

Bob Fu said, "The seminary school is in Los Angeles, and there's a Christian family waiting for you to stay with them – and Mid-Cities Church has committed to support you."

Just as I was settling into my Midland life, I faced an abrupt change – a move to a new city away from what had become familiar to me. I prayed, "Lord, Your will for me is abundantly clear. Although it appears I have mountains of gold and hills of silver right here in Midland, I will gladly surrender all of this to follow You."

Now I had to go to the apartment manager to inform him of my change of plans. I marched up to his office and let him know I would be leaving and heading to California. They were shocked! "It wasn't easy landing this apartment you now enjoy. Wait for a while," he said. "Maybe you'll stay?"

"No," I said. " God has called me to seminary, and if I come back here, it will only be to visit. Thank you for all you've done. You've been so nice to me."

I packed up my simple belongings, and we drove across Texas, New Mexico, and Arizona in two days in a U-Haul truck. While the trip itself was grueling, I couldn't help but marvel at the changing landscape of this vast land. Finally, we crossed the California border, bound for Los Angeles. My journey continued – California! Here I come!

WHAT DO YOU THINK?

What do you presently treasure that could make it difficult for you to follow His direction? What mountains of gold or hills of silver exist in your life that could stand in the way?

TODAY'S REFLECTION

_____
_____
_____
_____
_____
_____
_____
_____
_____
_____
_____
_____
_____

TODAY'S PRAYER

_____
_____
_____
_____
_____
_____
_____

DAY 24

Sarah Meets the Romeros

*A father to the fatherless, a defender of widows,
is God in his holy dwelling. God sets the lonely in
families, he leads out the prisoners with singing;
but the rebellious live in a sun-scorched land.*
(Psalm 68:5-6)

"Not possible," my friends forewarned. "It's just not possible for an American family to take you in for such a long time and for free. Not possible!" Although I didn't know this American family who vowed to take me in for four years, my confidence was in the Lord. Whoever these people were, God picked them out for me and me for them.

What made this arrangement all the more unbelievable for me was that in my Chinese background and experience, families simply didn't open their doors to strangers. Other family, yes. But strangers, no. Yet I had an inner peace from God that all would be well. My well-meaning friends seemed to think otherwise.

To begin with, let me say that the Romeros – Pastor Eddie, Rosie, and Grandpa – made a significant contribution to my journey in the Lord, and I'm eternally grateful to God for them.

They were a healing balm in my difficult life. Laughter and joy were a part of our daily lives together.

Think about it. I am Chinese, Pastor Eddie and his dad are Mexican, and his wife (Rosie) is Irish. We poked fun at ourselves and declared that God has a real sense of humor putting us together. One of our family customs was to read the Bible after breakfast. One morning, we read *Do not mistreat or oppress a foreigner, for you were foreigners in Egypt* (Exodus 22:21). After reading this in Exodus, I often brought up this text when I wanted my way or when I felt Pastor Eddie was getting too pushy. I'd just raise my hand and point my finger and say, "Don't oppress the foreigner!" Then we'd laugh. Our home was lighthearted and loving. As I said before, it was a healing experience for me.

When we pulled the U-Haul into the Romeros' driveway on our arrival, Grandpa (Ye Ye) Romero was the first to greet us. I surprised him by calling him by the affectionate title of Grandpa. He asked me, "How did you know I was Grandpa?"

"Bob Fu told us that's what everybody calls you." He smiled. I said, "All of us in Midland know your story – about you being in China during World War II as a U.S. Marine helping to extract the Japanese from our country."

The fact that this good report about his military past was still circulated pleased him. I went on to say, "And we heard that while you were in China, you had a Chinese girlfriend – that you like Chinese people." Mild surprise washed across his face as he laughed aloud while I shared the whole story as told by Bob Fu. To this day, that story is still circulated, accompanied by howls of delight from all our Chinese friends.

Rosie (Mom) came out and hurried us to the dinner table for a hot meal she'd prepared for our arrival. Pastor Eddie was on a ministry trip in Europe and would be home in a couple of weeks. In the meantime, the Romeros family offered immediate, palpable love, and my heart was at total peace.

Since my American English was still extremely poor and the Romeros knew no Chinese, we all depended heavily on hand motions and our own made-up sign language. How we communicated at all was only by the grace of God. Little by little, we became familiar with each other. Not only did my American English quickly improve, but they also started to master Chin-glish.

Mom was all in for birthdays and, when mine came around, she made a big thing about it. It had been so long since I had celebrated my birthday, and now it was a big thing! My birthday party included cake with candles, ice cream, gifts, and lots of fun, and it filled me with the joy of a child. It meant more than they could have ever imagined. Mom always made things so special. She has the touch of love and grace.

My first Christmas with the Romeros was both awkward and deeply meaningful. Early in December, Pastor Eddie and Grandpa went out to buy a Christmas tree. I wasn't quite sure exactly why they were doing this, or what it meant. But I could see in their faces that this was supposed to be done because it was Christmas time. The tree was pruned, the stand set up in the house, and they carried the tree inside. Mom and Pastor went into the garage and brought in storage boxes full of decorations from Christmases past. To my surprise, Pastor Eddie opened a box with Christmas lights – like the ones I'd made while in prison. I gasped at the sight. "I made those!" I exclaimed.

Pastor Eddie paused with a look of confusion. "You made what?"

"Those." I pointed to the string of Christmas lights in his hands. "I made those lights, in prison."

Pastor Eddie slowly unwound the string of lights, and read the tag. He still looked a bit stunned as he showed it to me.

They were without a doubt made in China. An awkwardness hung in the air. Hmm, what now? He plugged them in, and they failed to turn on. "I made that one," I said. And we erupted in laughter, which chased away any bit of uneasiness remaining.

By the end of the evening, our home was transformed into Christmas. A fire blazed in the hearth, and the spectacular tree stood decorated, amidst the living room draped with garland and lit with candles. When we turned off all the lights, I'll never forget the feeling of Christmas wonder as it fell upon us. Tears brimmed in my eyes as I beheld the beauty dedicated to Jesus.

Now that I knew what the lights were for, I was reminded of that Bible passage where Joseph tells his brothers, *You intended to harm me, but God intended it for good to accomplish what is now being done* (Genesis 50:20). The harsh work at the labor camps of making Christmas lights was to line the pockets of corrupt officials and businessmen, but God used it to bless us with beauty and wonder, celebrating the incarnation of His Son. Today, I still tell people that the best thing they could do when they put up their Christmas lights is not to be angry, even though there is plenty of indignation to go around, but rather to remember to pray for those sisters and brothers still in prison forced to do this labor. Turn your anger into intercession when you see "Made in China."

On the morning of December 25, the Romeros shared a breakfast of tamales with eggs. When we finished, we moved into the living room to open gifts. First, I opened my gift from Pastor Eddie. It was a beautiful long velvet bag filled with quarters. By this time, I had my own car, and Pastor Eddie washed all the family cars on Friday at the quarter car wash. So, instead of me giving him quarters for the machine, he had provided quarters to last me a long time. Mom and Pastor Eddie were always thoughtful like that, but it was Grandpa who was exceedingly generous and caring toward me in his own quiet way. Time and space available in this chapter don't allow me to express the many blessings the Romeros showered on me, but I must share one last recollection before I move on.

Friday nights were my hot-pot cooking nights. After dinner, we had Bible reading, discussion, and prayer. I was asked, "How did you pray in China?" I explained to the Romeros that we would always pray on our knees as we cried out to God. Grandpa said, "Then we too will pray on our knees." These were faith-building amazing times. Especially when Grandpa (eighty-something) struggled to get down on his knees. Pastor Eddie even told him he didn't have to do that. Grandpa said, "It's the least I can do for our great God!" There was no arguing that point. To this day, I can still see him struggling to get on his knees. His example lives on, even though he has gone home to the Lord.

My life was restored and rebuilt at the Romeros'. Joy and hope were my companions, thanks to my God, who placed me in *this* family.

WHAT DO YOU THINK?

Self-isolation and estrangement isn't God's plan for our life –
families are. Why not take some time to express appreciation
for your family or church family?

TODAY'S REFLECTION

_____

_____

_____

_____

_____

_____

_____

_____

_____

_____

_____

_____

_____

TODAY'S PRAYER

_____

_____

_____

_____

_____

_____

_____

_____

PART 6

AMERICA, MY BLUE SKY

DAY 25

Skyping with My Parents

Now to him who is able to do immeasurably more than all we ask or imagine, according to his power that is at work within us, to him be glory in the church and in Christ Jesus throughout all generations, for ever and ever! Amen. (Ephesians 3:20-21)

When I reached America, I couldn't wait to call my parents back in China. "Baba, Mama, I'm in America!" On the other end of the line, my news was met with strong skepticism.

"How can that be?" my father asked. I could hear utter disbelief in his voice. My mom remained quiet. I knew she believed me.

My father tried to support his skepticism by challenging me to the reasonableness of my claim that I was in America. "We have no one in America, no family, no friends, no one!" He doubled down in his unbelief.

Mixed emotions fought within me. I knew it was no good trying to explain the unexplainable to him. At that moment, he was unable to think or imagine what God had done. My life in America was so completely foreign to him, and much too complicated to explain over the phone. As a result, they continued to worry about my health, safety, and well-being.

One day my cousin was listening to an illegal radio station, Voice of America (VOA) radio, a satellite radio station. The news segment he heard came from Washington, D.C., where I was being interviewed by the VOA reporter, after testifying before a congressional committee. He recognized my voice and, in his excitement, he rushed to my parents' home to tell them what he had heard. "Little sister is in America! She is on the radio! She really is in America!" You might think my father would come around once my true whereabouts had been independently verified, but my cousin's report only garnered more skepticism.

Baba said, "I wish she was in America, but that's impossible." He then laid out his rationale for his unbelief. "She would need lots of money to go to America, and I know she doesn't even have a bank account, let alone any money to deposit."

I'm not sure why my father was so bent on not believing the report. Was it to protect himself from an impossible hope? God only knows. Again, my mother quietly accepted all of these notices in loving faith in Christ. She knew our God could do *immeasurably more than all we ask or imagine* (Ephesians 3:20).

At the start of my second year in the U.S., I lived in Los Angeles with my American family, the Romeros. Although I attended seminary, I wanted to work to earn money too, in order to hopefully one day return to my beloved China and see my family again. My mind constantly went back to my family and China. One day a family member in China contacted me, and we arranged a Skype meeting with my parents. Now they will believe that I am in America! I thought.

The date and time was set. It was evening time in Los Angeles, near 7:00 p.m., which would be near 10:00 a.m. the next day in China. Everything was ready. Baba and Mama sat in front of the computer at my brother's house, and we, Pastor Eddie, Mom (Rosie), Grandpa, and me, patiently waited for the link to connect.

Finally, the computer's cameras came to life. With the link established, the moment I'd waited for arrived. There on the computer screen were my mom and dad. My heart filled with excitement as we exchanged greetings. I was thrilled to be able to convince them that I was really in America, and that I was well and well cared for. I translated for the Romeros, and I turned to introduce Grandpa (Ye Ye). Grandpa stood in front of the laptop and greeted my parents. I translated for them. Though my father was hard to read, a subtle change came over him. How could he deny I was in America now? The proof was undeniable. Mom faithfully sat at my dad's side taking it all in.

Next, I introduced Mom (Rosie) to my mom and dad. With her light hair, blue eyes, and fair skin, there was no denying I was in America. My mom and dad sat directly in front of the camera, yet I could see my other family members in the background. They were happy and excited to meet Mom. I could hear them chattering in the background, as we ourselves were animated on our end. Lastly, I introduced Pastor Eddie, and for this part, I will let him describe the event in his own words.

In Pastor Eddie's Words

"It's an honor to finally meet all of you," I said. "I want to let you know your daughter is safe and well in America. We love having her here with us and thank God for putting us all together. Now, I want Sarah to walk you through our home so you can see she is well provided for and you have nothing to worry about."

At this point, I asked Sarah to take my laptop and do a walk through our home – the dining room, kitchen, TV room, hallway, and her bedroom. Here Sarah took time to describe thoughtfully everything in her room, starting with the big stuffed animals on her bed. Finally, she walked back down the hall and into the living room. "Show them the fireplace," I said. And with that, our tour was complete.

Then I turned to Sarah and said, "Now, I want you to translate everything I'm about to say and don't leave anything out – okay?"

She nodded. "Okay."

I turned to face the laptop camera and said, "As you can see, we have many things in our home. Many things that we love and treasure." Sarah translated. They were all fixed on her translation. The tone took on an atmosphere of importance. "This computer we are talking on was made in China, a very good computer." Sarah translated, while her parents and family looked on. "This wristwatch, made in China, also very good quality." Sarah translated. "This furniture made in China too, very good," I said. By this time, the redundancy was picked up on, but they weren't sure where this was all going. In fact, Sarah looked perplexed with where I was taking this. "Finally," I said, "we have many beautiful and wonderful things in our home, but none is more excellent than your daughter. She too was made in China." Sarah turned to me unable to speak, so overwhelmed with the compliment. Once she composed herself, she translated what I said.

I reminded her, "Word for word!" Through tears of joy and the glorious presence of the Lord, she got through the translation. Happiness and peace came over the entire family, including her parents, as they understood the compliment.

"We now know she is in good hands," her parents said. And with many other words, they expressed deep gratitude for our love and care for their daughter.

This was one of those rare holy moments that will never be forgotten at the Romero home. After we wrapped up our Skype meeting and said our good-byes, we just basked quietly in the goodness of God.

WHAT DO YOU THINK?

Can you recall a time when you tried to express the work of Christ in your life to the skeptical or disbelieving? Perhaps your testimony can bring a skeptic one giant step closer to the kingdom's door.

TODAY'S REFLECTION

_____
_____
_____
_____
_____
_____
_____
_____
_____
_____
_____
_____
_____
_____

TODAY'S PRAYER

_____
_____
_____
_____
_____
_____
_____

DAY 26

My Citizenship

*But our citizenship is in heaven. And we eagerly
await a Savior from there, the Lord Jesus Christ.*
(Philippians 3:20)

One morning as I sat around the breakfast table with the Romeros, I blurted out, "I've made a decision." Grandpa, Mom, and Pastor Eddie all stared at me as if I were ready to make some monumental announcement. "I will pick a Bible name when I become an American citizen."

"Can you do that?" Pastor Eddie asked.

"Yes," I replied. "Every new citizen has one opportunity to change their name for free."

Mom asked, "Have you thought of a name or shall we all give suggestions?"

"Well," I said as I thoughtfully moved the food around on my plate for a second and then looked up at them. "I kind of like the name Jael, what do you think?"

Grandpa asked, "Where in the Bible is Jael?"

Pastor Eddie said, "Isn't she the woman who took in Sisera, the fleeing commander of the Canaanite army?"

"Yes, that's her!" I said with excitement. "She was so bold and courageous!"

Grandpa nodded slightly. "Oh yeah, she's the woman who drove a stake through the general's temple, and gained the honor for the victory."

"That's right." I couldn't help but smile with delight. Pastor Eddie said something under his breath. "What was that?" I asked.

"Well," he said, "I'd be afraid to lay my head down with someone in my house named Jael!"

We all laughed, but as the laughter faded, I thought, But I like that name. Is Pastor Eddie joking, as he does so often, or is there something unbecoming of that name? It made me pause and rethink what name I should adopt. This opened me up to other possibilities.

Not long afterwards, at another breakfast time, I said, "What about Abigail?"

"For your new name?" Mom asked.

"Yes, she was a good woman."

"Wise and beautiful," Grandpa added.

Pastor Eddie mused, "Hmmm, Abigail? Do you like the name?"

"Yes, very much."

"I think we are all in agreement then. Abigail fits you well!"

For me it was settled. My name was Abigail.[11]

A Word About My Citizenship

In America, I've found a desperate and aggressive inclination toward U.S. citizenship in Chinese communities. By *desperate*, I mean individuals and families dream of coming to America as the land of freedom and opportunity. The greatest country on earth. A country where people have an equal opportunity to succeed and get ahead. Where corruption is not the norm and opportunity isn't limited to the rich.

11 Sarah Liu is a pen name. However, Abigail Romero Chang is my true legal name. Because I have used Sarah Liu much longer than I have had Abigail, to eliminate confusion with my audiences, I have kept continuity by using Sarah Liu.

By *aggressive*, I mean that the open door of travel to and from China may be limited and citizenship must be obtained now while the door is open. Tragically, I've met many of my own people who will go to any and every measure to gain this citizenship. I have witnessed fraudulent claims of religious persecution to gain refugee status in order to gain the path to citizenship. In this regard, I considered myself blessed of God, strangely enough, that I never had to connive and lie my way through the immigration process. My persecution is well documented. In fact, I obtained my refugee status while still in Thailand. The U.S. government, officials, and congressmen took great interest in my case, with much thanks due to Bob Fu.

Here, I boasted in the Lord for what He had done for me. In prison and in freedom, I will boast of His great love and kindness to me – Abigail.

With my green card in hand, I took the necessary steps to complete the citizenship process. Finally, the day of my citizenship arrived. On that weekday morning, we all awoke early to get ready for my big day. It was a warm, sunny day in Los Angeles. Because Pastor Eddie and Mom's daughter Sarah and son-in-law Scott Yetter lived only one block from the Los Angeles Convention Center, at the corner of Figueroa and Pico, we parked at their house and walked to the center.

Thousands of people flowed into the convention center, and excitement and joy filled the air. Mom and I dressed up for the occasion. Afterwards, we all planned to have breakfast at the famous Original Pantry Cafe on Figueroa Street.

At long last, the ceremony began. All of the new citizens sat at the front of the auditorium, with our family and friends seated in the back. Pastor Eddie, Mom, and I kept ourselves in eye view the whole time. The lights dimmed and a video of President Obama welcomed us as the newest members of the

U.S. Then, the sacred moment came – the taking of the oath of citizenship.

We were all asked to stand and to raise our right hand. How solemn the atmosphere became. You could hear a pin drop, except for the occasional baby crying. I have included part of the oath of citizenship because most Americans, born here, never had to take the oath. It is a lofty oath:

> *I hereby declare, on oath, that I absolutely and entirely renounce and abjure all allegiance and fidelity to any foreign prince, potentate, State, or sovereignty, and particularly to _____ of who or which I have heretofore been a subject or citizen; that I will support and defend the Constitution and laws of the United States of America against all enemies, foreign and domestic; ... and that I take this obligation freely, without any mental reservation or purpose of evasion;* **so help me God**. [emphasis added]

I wanted to shout that last clause, "so help me God." We would have never made such an oath in China ending with "so help me God." Communists are atheists. The state is above all; it is "so help me Mao."

All families were excused to go outside and wait for their loved ones as they finalized and signed the remaining document. I saw Pastor Eddie and Mom step out of their seats and I waved to them. Soon, I found myself finalizing my citizenship. At one of the stations, they asked, "Will you change your name?"

"Yes," I happily replied.

"Please fill out this form and your name will be official."

As I prepared to exit the convention center, we were directed to a certain door. I stepped outside looking for Mom and Pastor Eddie. Our pathway was roped off and family and friends stood on either side of the barrier. Then I spotted Mom and Pastor Eddie in the large crowd. "Let's see your citizenship!" Pastor Eddie called out. I proudly opened my beautiful folder and showed them my citizenship document with my new first name and my new last name.

Mom and Pastor Eddie were speechless. Finally, Mom spoke up and said, "We knew about changing your first name, but you took on our family last name too."

Pastor Eddie was overwhelmed with honor and joy. "I never saw this coming. I am so proud to have you share our name. Wait till Grandpa sees this!"

As wonderful and monumental as this moment was for me – long before I landed on the shores of America, while still in China – I made an oath to Jesus Christ. He who is above all nations and kingdoms. I promised to be loyal to Him, and Him alone, so help me God. My ultimate citizenship is in heaven, and I await my Savior to return to take me HOME.

WHAT DO YOU THINK?

As Christians, we have a dual citizenship – one in heaven and one on earth. Which realm are you closer to? Where do your ultimate loyalties lie?

TODAY'S REFLECTION

_____
_____
_____
_____
_____
_____
_____
_____
_____
_____
_____
_____
_____

TODAY'S PRAYER

_____
_____
_____
_____
_____
_____
_____

DAY 27

My Wedding Day

"Hallelujah! For our Lord God Almighty reigns. Let us rejoice and be glad and give him glory! For the wedding of the Lamb has come, and his bride has made herself ready. Fine linen, bright and clean, was given her to wear." (Revelation 19:6b-8)

Oone of the most important days in the future will be a wedding unlike any other. This wedding will celebrate Jesus Christ, the groom, and His bride, the church. Along with this, there will be a banquet. No matter how grand the weddings or how extravagant the banquets we have here on earth, they are nothing but shadows of what that day will be like when we Christians celebrate the blessed hope.

My wedding day here on earth exceeded all my expectations. How much more so will the day be when we are united with Him for all eternity.

For this chapter, I have asked key friends to share their memories of my glorious wedding day here on earth. The following are their own words:

Bob Fu: Officiator

[Sarah] a persecuted church leader from China. A refugee

rescued through my "Underground Railroad." Now a beautiful, shy bride waiting for yet another big moment in her life. That was July 11, 2011, at Sarah Liu's wedding with her groom, Josh.

I was honored to be the pastor to officiate at her wedding and to preach the message of covenantal love for this new, godly young family. Her newly adopted father, Pastor Eddie Romero, escorted her down the aisle and handed her over to Josh after I asked, "Who gives this woman?"

I witnessed something spectacular in the room. The sanctuary was almost full and included men and women, pastors and laymen, young and old, black, white, and yellow skin, with voices speaking in different languages: Chinese, Spanish, and English. But they all held one thing in common – the transcendent love of Christ, which bound this whole thing together.

Sarah was abused and tortured during her six years in a labor camp for her dedication to the heavenly groom, Christ, and the bride, His church. Now she stood, as the bride, with her groom ready to build a family on earth. A new phase of exciting life with challenges, which offer a foretaste of what's coming in the heavenly consummation when the wedding of the Lamb of God is performed. *They triumphed over him by the blood of the Lamb and by the word of their testimony; they did not love their lives so much as to shrink from death* (Revelation 12:11).

I pronounced the blessings upon Sarah and Josh as husband and wife, while inwardly I thought, O Lord, You are so amazing. Sarah's Christ-centered triumph through her trail of blood and testimonies has already touched hundreds of thousands of people of God around the globe. She is now raised as part of this troop of overcomers by the word of her testimony, and only You can orchestrate this new page of her life providentially.

May the Lord continue to mold them in this intimate relationship to experience what Christ and His church have modeled – the eternal love and obedience for the utmost glory of our heavenly Father.

Joshua Chang: Groom

"Your family will join our wedding day?" Sarah asked me.

I said, "They would like to. Probably they can't. My father is staying in the hospital for his lung cancer [in Taiwan]. But my uncle and my aunt will come."

Sarah looked at me with compassion and said, "My family in China won't have enough time to undertake all necessary procedures for obtaining passports and visas. But we have a big American church family here. We will see how God will bless us through our wedding day."

I was so honored that this milestone, our wedding day, would soon arrive. I wanted to do my best in planning for our wedding ceremony, but I knew neither of us could do it alone. So, when Pastor Eddie and the HCF family volunteered to help plan our wedding day, I was deeply grateful for their loving heart.

When the wedding ceremony began, I had expected a small turnout. Instead, I couldn't believe my eyes. So many friends attended! The church was full, and each person brought their blessing for us on that day.

The theme and decor for our wedding ceremony and reception was *cool ocean summer breeze*. All our friends had joyful smiles. The fragrance of candles on the table filled the air and each table displayed beautiful shells. So many details to describe – the big tower wedding cake, the romantic songs, the beautiful picture galleries, and delicious food. Everything was perfect.

When my beautiful bride, Sarah, walked in, escorted by Pastor Eddie, she amazed me. In fact, she reminded me of the bride of Christ. *And to present her to himself as a radiant church, without stain or wrinkle of any other blemish, but holy and blameless* (Ephesians 5:27). And, as Sarah and I said our vows and lit the unity candle, we were united as one, to start our new journey in Jesus Christ.

The wedding festivities came to an end, but the blessings of that special day – the fellowship with our friends, and the HCF family, and the Romeros – still continue.

God is good, all the time.

Qiao Hong: Maid of Honor

It was my privilege to be Sarah's maid of honor. We were good friends and had been classmates at seminary school. Her wedding day was unforgettable. God had set aside this special day for her and her husband, and I was filled with gratitude and joy and praise to our God.

When the music of the "Wedding March" sounded, she walked slowly into the hall with Pastor Eddie and down the aisle. Excitement filled me. I couldn't believe that the scene in front of me was really happening. My friend Sarah was getting married to Joshua. The Lord had done great things for her with blessings flowing like the streams in the Negev. We couldn't stop cheering. *Those who sow with tears will reap with songs of joy* (Psalm 126:5). Wasn't today a harvest day for her? Wasn't today her *cheering* day?

Even though her parents couldn't participate in the wedding in person, the church was still full of so many brothers and sisters, and they all witnessed the great things which the Lord had done for my sister Sarah.

As I stood there, I remembered how she had paid the price for the gospel, had been in prison, and had experienced a bitter life as she devoted her youth to the Lord, without a thought of marriage. I thought, She is trained to focus on His kingdom. Her face is veiled, and I can't see her beauty, except for two wet lines painted by tears streaming down her face. Her hands are hidden. I can't see the effects of moisturizing skincare. She had often gone without food, with much fasting. This was the life she lived before the Lord. But . . . just look at her now.

On her wedding day, I sobbed for joy. Is there anything impossible for our God who unfolds this scene before my very eyes? Who has her walk on the red carpet? Who prepared her lifelong partner? It is the Lord whom she serves with her life. The Lord made this wedding a miracle, as certain as Jesus changed water to wine. How wonderful it is.

I sincerely looked forward to her book, knowing her testimony would spread to the ends of the earth. No matter who reads this book, I pray that *those who are wise will shine like the brightness of the heavens, and those who lead many to righteousness, like the stars for ever and ever* (Daniel 12:3). Amen!

Mom Rosie and Grandpa Romero's Prayer

About Grandpa (Ye Ye)
Grandpa Romero grew to love Sarah as she quickly became a part of our household. He was there to help her, especially during those first few months in our home. Oftentimes, he was the one who drove her to Bible school and any other places she needed to go. He became her American "Ye Ye." Their combined sense of humor gave our home an atmosphere of joy and laughter. She loved to sneak up on Grandpa, as he napped on the couch, and tickle his ear with a feather.

He was extremely honored when Sarah and Joshua asked him to pray over them as part of the wedding ceremony. Grandpa didn't take this assignment lightly. Before the wedding, he prayed and considered what words would truly glorify God. When the moment arrived, a profound sense of holiness brought tears to many, including the bride and groom. His prayer of blessing still covers Sarah and Joshua like a warm blanket of love.

Mom Rosie

When asked to share something about Sarah's wedding day, the picture that came to mind was our front door. Five years earlier, she walked through our door ready to start a new page of her life. She showed such courage and dependence on God. Before the wedding ceremony, she once again walked through that same door. She had about fifteen minutes before she had to arrive at church in her wedding dress. Her face shined with the grace of God. It was as if a few more pieces of her life puzzle had fallen into place. It was a day I will always remember.

Liu Xianxiu: Sarah's Sister and Witness through Skype

My dear younger sister always told me by phone, "Don't worry about me. My heavenly Father always sends angels around me. I'm happy and enjoy my life in America."

As she is the youngest one of our siblings, and she is far away from us, all of our family misses her and worries about her even though she has told us she is doing well. Deep down in our hearts, we still think she is a baby. On her special wedding day, through Skype, we saw her walk into the beautiful wedding ceremony with her guardian, Pastor Eddie. Suddenly, she was not a baby to us anymore, but a beautiful bride. I was so emotional, with tears wetting my face because of all the memories that flooded back to me: She was so cute when she was a child, and naughty when she was a youth. She was so brave to follow Jesus. Now look at her – the most beautiful bride.

When I saw the elegant church filled with friends, I recalled how she would often say that she had a big American family. We were so proud of her, and our hearts were comforted. We had no worries. Our parents and siblings want to say, "Praise Jesus Christ!" And a big thank-you to all her friends. You did for our younger sister more than enough.

"Romeros, we can't express how grateful we are for what you did for my sister Sarah. But we can say, your love shows your faith. We are one body in Christ."

Reggie Littlejohn: Honored Guest

I remember sitting in my backyard on a sunny day in California and reading on the Internet about the horrific story of torture and religious persecution of Sarah Liu. The Chinese government did so many things to her, including jumping on her hands. She was with Bob Fu, testifying at a Voice of the Martyrs conference. In the photo, she looked so beautiful, so fragile, so pure. I couldn't imagine how anyone could do such things to her. The thought of it filled me with righteous indignation, and it also made me weep.

Months later, my husband, Rob, and I were attending a VOM conference. I heard a beautiful young woman testifying about her persecution in China. Suddenly, I realized it was the same person I'd read about. I turned to my husband and said, "That's HER. That's the woman I told you about."

After her testimony, I approached her and said how much her testimony meant to me. I asked her how she could withstand so much torture for such a long time and not "break" – telling the authorities information that would get her fellow Christians in trouble.

She replied, "We worship a mighty God."

The worst part of her torture for me was when they jumped on her hands. I couldn't imagine the pain. With her permission, I kissed her hands. Then I took off my favorite watch and put it on her wrist, saying, "Every time you look at this watch, remember that I am praying for you."

The next time we met was in Midland, Texas. We were going out to lunch with a mutual friend. I went to her room to tell her it was time to go and gently opened the door. She was kneeling by her bed, praying, with tears streaming down her face. I asked her why she was crying and she said that the Chinese government had just kidnapped some Christians, and she was worried that they were being tortured. Her love and empathy for persecuted Christians in China deeply impressed me. I felt she was a spiritual giant.

But this little "giant" also had practical needs. I asked her how I could support her in prayer. She asked me to pray for her to get a car. I started praying for this, and within a short time, someone donated a car for her use. She said, "Clearly, God answers your prayers," and so she gave me a more important prayer request: "Pray that I find a husband."

I began praying for the Lord to lead her to a compassionate, godly man to be her husband. Within a short time, she found Joshua.

The wedding was such a joyful occasion with so many who loved Sarah and Joshua gathered around to bless them. Sarah, of course, was gorgeous. I could hardly believe the Lord had lifted up this precious sister from a torture chamber in China to this beautiful wedding in California. Our God is a God of healing and restoration. As Sarah had said to me years before, "We worship a mighty God."

Helen Aguilar: HCF Wedding Team Leader

I praised and thanked God for bringing Joshua and Sarah to La Puente, California, from the other side of the world – to meet, fall in love, and be blessed with the gift of marriage. God was glorified.

> "For I know the plans I have for you," declares
> the LORD, "plans to prosper you and not to
> harm you, plans to give you hope and a future."
> (Jeremiah 29:11)

Joshua and Sarah's wedding was truly a blessing from God. A great joy was present at the wedding planning meetings. The team met and worked with Joshua and Sarah in preparation for that big day. Our meetings were filled with lots of laughter, fellowship, and good food. God was glorified.

Rejoice with those who rejoice. (Romans 12:15a)

During the wedding ceremony, there were several special moments, including Pastor Bob Fu officiating the wedding, Papa Romero praying a blessing over them, Pastor Eddie giving Sarah's hand in marriage, and Ella Carrillo singing praises to God for this joyful occasion. Among these special moments, I also have to mention how Jason Tucker connected us all through Skype. Sarah's parents and family from China watched the wedding ceremony and were able to send their love and best wishes. Truly, God was glorified.

Sarah: The Bride

My wedding day was only one day, but God's grace and the memory of my friends' blessings will continue for all my life. The profound truth is that we are indeed one body in Christ, and we, the bride of Christ, will enter into the eternal union with Jesus Christ our Lord. Amen.

WHAT DO YOU THINK?

Making a covenant with another person is a major life undertaking. I stand in awe and wonder that the God of the universe has given His Son to the lowly of this earth. He is the eternal groom, and we the eternal bride. Are you as awestruck by that thought as I am?

TODAY'S REFLECTION

_____

_____

_____

_____

_____

_____

_____

_____

_____

_____

_____

_____

TODAY'S PRAYER

_____

_____

_____

_____

_____

_____

DAY 28

Where the Spiritual and the Practical Meet

So do not worry, saying, 'What shall we eat?' or
'What shall we drink?' or 'What shall we wear?'
But seek first his kingdom and his righteousness,
and all these things will be given to you as well.
(Matthew 6:31, 33)

While I was in China, ministering as an evangelist, God proved Himself faithful in every way. Even in the dark days of prison and the labor camp, His light of loving provision shined as a witness to all. But now I was in America, a dramatically different world from my rural China. I was never a big-city girl. Simple needs were easily obtained through prayer and the kindness of my sisters, brothers, and, on occasion, total strangers.

Coming to America was entirely different. For me, the environment in Texas and California posed new challenges I never imagined while in the gospel field in China. Now, the conventional wisdom of all my new American friends seemed to be "Everybody needs a car to get around." Over and over, they'd tell me, "Sarah, you need a car."

A car? I wondered. In China, my prayers were for a coat, a place to lay my head, and a warm meal. Now I need a car? This request seemed so big. My faith was challenged American style . . . a car.

Please understand, this is not really about cars; it is about the One who provides for us. Whether it's our next meal or our next car. To help you understand what I mean, let me trace the footsteps of God's provision of cars to meet my needs.

My First Car

My first car was a 1980-something Honda Accord, which I received when I lived in Midland, Texas. In an earlier chapter, I wrote about the kindness and patience of Uncle Doug and Sister Jean, who taught me how to drive. After three tries at my written test, I finally passed and received my permit allowing me to get behind the wheel of a real car. At that point, I put Uncle Doug and Sister Jean to the test, and they proved to be *real* Christians. The scene was comical. Uncle Doug, a very big man, sat next to me – a very small woman. Both of us struggled to communicate and drive all at the same time. Truly, God was with us.

Then came the actual driving test. To make a long story short, I failed the first and second behind-the-wheel tests. I guess you could best describe me as discouraged but determined. I went for my third and final chance to pass. At the end of my test, the driving examiner handed me another form that had English words on it. I took my form and handed it to my Chinese friend Joshua. He said, "You passed!" Oh, what joy!

Once I had my license, my American friends often asked, "Now that you have your license, what about a car?"

My answer was always the same. "I'll pray, and God will provide."

After some time, a dear Christian couple from Taiwan invited me out for lunch. They asked, "Do you have a car?"

I said, "I am praying for one."

"We have a used Honda we'd like to give to you." Joy rushed into my soul as I silently prayed, "Lord, You answered my prayer." It is hard to explain the depth of gratitude I felt to God and these lovely servants at that moment. Moments like these were faith builders for me, in a new land where things were very different. The one constant was our great God – truly the Lord of the whole earth. After lunch, they drove the car to my apartment. I was ready to become mobile.

My Second Car

I received my second car in Los Angeles, California. It was a 1998 Nissan Altima, although, since the letter "i" was missing, it made mine an Alt_ma. I enjoyed the privilege of driving my Honda for about one year, and it was so helpful. I discovered a new level of independence. Driving my humble, used Honda was like a dream, and it offered a physical and practical reminder of the Lord's kindness. Here I was, a small-town country girl from China, driving in my own car in the great land of America – blue skies only God could provide.

When the time had arrived for me to leave the comforts of Midland, Texas, to head to the unknowns God was calling me to in Los Angeles, I passed on the blessing of my Honda to a Chinese couple and left for Los Angeles. What awaited me I wasn't certain, and again, my God was the only constant.

Once I arrived in the big city of Los Angeles, it was so much different from Midland. I found myself in need of a car more than ever before. I thought, If God is in Midland, God is in Los Angeles too. Once again, I prayed, "Abba Father, my earthly father cannot buy me a car, but You, my heavenly Father, can help me. All cars on the earth belong to You. If it is Your will, please do this for me."

A few days later, I received a $2,500 check. I stared at the check in my hand, stunned by what I *thought* it said. I read it over and over again, until the realization came over me that this IS God's provision, like money from heaven.

The amount of the check astonished me, and then I looked at the name of the contributor. I didn't recognize the person's name but was thankful nevertheless. I sat down immediately to write a thank-you card to them, expressing my most sincere gratitude. After penning these words, I lovingly placed the card in the envelope, addressed the card to the person on the check, and sent it off.

Once I deposited the check, the search for a new used car began. About five days later, my thank-you card returned with "No such person" scrawled on the envelope. "What?" I said to myself. "I have the money, but there's no such person?"

I doubled checked the name and address on the check and confirmed it was correct. How confusing. This doesn't make sense. This had to be a real person who donated to my needs. So, I decided to call the phone number listed on the check. I called several times, only to have no one answer. Frustrated, I dialed the number one last time. It was ringing. How many times should I let it ring? Okay, one more ring. To my surprise, a man answered the phone. I immediately identified myself and started to express my gratitude when he cut me off with "I don't know what you're talking about; you have the wrong person." Click. I stared at the phone in my hand, unsure of what to think. I double checked the phone number listed on the check. I had dialed correctly. I had no logical explanation for all of this. For me, it boiled down to one fact: God can do anything, any way. I thought about how the Lord paid taxes with coins from the fish's mouth. Money for my car from a stranger or an angel is in keeping with His mysterious work.

What I did next may sound like I'm a bit spoiled by my heavenly Father, but I prayed, "Lord, twenty-five hundred dollars is a good start for a good used car, but I need more. I know I will never be put to shame when I depend on You."

My American Uncle Doug called me from Texas and sent me a check for $3,500, and I asked Pastor Eddie to help me buy a used car. I have more to say about this in the next section.

My Third Car

My third car was a brand-new 2016 Toyota Corolla. I had owned my Nissan for about nine years. That's a long time to own a used car. I kept up with the maintenance every year and was forced to make many repairs during that time. I said, "I hate pouring money into my car."

But my guardian reminded me over and over again, "If you keep up with the maintenance and fix things the moment you detect them, the car will last you a long, long time."

I reluctantly heeded his counsel and tried to keep up the car. Finally, I had enough. "What? Another thousand-dollar repair?"

My guardian said, "Here are the choices you have. You can continue making repairs as needed and have no monthly payments and very low insurance premiums, or you can get a new car and have the peace of mind of no annual repairs, at least for a good while, but you'll have a monthly payment and higher insurance premiums. What would you like to do?"

My guardian is very good at laying out my options, but he leaves the decision-making to me. "Lord, help me!" I cried. "I'm not sure what to do."

Joshua and I talked about it, looked over the numbers, and decided to go for the new car. "Lord, this is the first real purchase we will be making on our own. I don't see a 'miracle' car on the horizon." Joshua gave me the okay, and I began researching the "best bang for my buck," as my American friends would say.

Before we decided to make an actual purchase, while we were still researching, the unthinkable happened. In the midst of stop-and-go traffic, during rush hour one night on one of the busiest freeways in L.A., my car overheated and stalled in the number-two lane. In a panic, I tried to restart it, without success. Steam or smoke billowed from under the hood. I put my flashers on and I didn't know what to do. Hundreds of cars started to back up, looking like ribbons of headlights trailing into the distance. Out of nowhere, emergency lights approached along the shoulder of the freeway.

What I'm about to explain may sound crazy and maybe I should be dead, but I waved frantically to the emergency vehicle and got out of my car and started walking across the freeway lanes. Just writing this down makes me think I was crazy. The emergency worker yelled at me to get back in my car, but I didn't understand him and continued to walk toward him. Exasperated, he got on his loudspeaker and commanded me to return to my car. The loudspeaker distorted his voice, but I was certain if I could just get to him I could explain my dilemma.

There I was, maneuvering through traffic on foot across the lanes and dodging cars to get to the worker. Finally, in his frantic attempt to get me to stay in my vehicle, I understood what he was saying. I turned around and maneuvered my way back to my car, got inside, and waited for him to bring his emergency vehicle into position. Traffic that night was a nightmare, and I only made matters worse.

Finally, the emergency worker towed me from the freeway, and I made a phone call to my guardian to figure out what to do next. The worker stayed with me until my guardian showed up. While I waited, I prayed, "Abba, Father, what do I do now?"

I spoke with Joshua, and he was adamant. "We need to buy you a new car. This must not happen again."

My guardian had the car towed to the mechanic's shop. The next day our mechanic declared the car "dead." The engine block was cracked and a score of other things needed repair. No more! The car was sold for $150. There I stood with $150 in my hand as they towed my car around the corner and out of sight. "Thank you, Lord, for supplying my needs. Help us to be wise in purchasing the next car."

My guardian explained everything involved in making a new car purchase. Joshua and I finally settled on a brand-new silver 2016 Toyota Corolla. But since neither of us had ever bought a new car, we wanted my guardian to test-drive the car before we made the purchase. After the test-drive, he said, "For the price, you have a good car with a good company. I like it, and God willing, you will have many years of good driving." Joshua and I took the plunge and have been happy with the car ever since.

What makes my God so amazing is that He is personal. I clearly see His hand and touch on even the basic and simple things of life. This isn't some sterile theological statement; this is the truth. God is concerned about even the smallest things in my life. I am thankful for the people He has placed in my life, but nobody or nothing is a substitute for who He is to me. He knows my heart, sees my needs, and works things out. Just like in China, I look to Him and He supplies what I need and more.

WHAT DO YOU THINK?

Can you recall the last time you were mindful of His loving provision in your life? Even the *common blessings* we all share? Now is a good time to say thanks . . . again.

TODAY'S REFLECTION

_____
_____
_____
_____
_____
_____
_____
_____
_____
_____
_____
_____
_____

TODAY'S PRAYER

_____
_____
_____
_____
_____
_____
_____
_____
_____

Missing My Mom, Reuniting with My Father

Children's children are a crown to the aged,
and parents are the pride of their children.
(Proverbs 17:6)

I have many friends, far and near, praying for me. My dream to visit my beloved China had become a reality. At the time of this writing, I was in China. It had been more than a decade since I'd escaped persecution in China, and by all reports, persecution had stepped up under the harsh treatment of the current President Xi Jinping. The harsh treatment had extended beyond the house-church movement and now included several Three Self Churches (government-registered churches).

I had shared my heart's burden to see my aged daddy (ninety-five years old) once again – to see his face, hold his hand, and look into his eyes and tell him of the great salvation that awaits him in Jesus Christ. God made a way for this to happen.

Missing My Mom

On Monday, November 14, 2016, United Airlines Flight 32 departed LAX for China at 10:50 a.m. In my mind, I was already in China – completely focused on the trip before me. This trip was the answer to the prayers of many, including me. We lifted off, and climbed higher into the sky toward my unknown destiny.

Some might ask, "Wasn't this trip a bit risky?" The answer is yes. But to me it was a risk worth taking in the Lord. Obtaining a visa from China (under my new name and as an American citizen) was a difficult task. But now airborne, the next moment of difficulty would be arriving in China and crossing customs and immigration successfully.

The discussion between me and the people close to me went something like this: "Perhaps they granted you a visa just to get you back in China where they can take you into custody?" Others said, "No, too much time has elapsed, they have bigger fish to fry!" Still others suggested, "Maybe this is the open door we have prayed for?"

In the end, it came down to God's peace regarding the direction I should go, and my heavy heart for my daddy. I knew the risks, and I knew my God. I walked by faith and trusted Him at every step.

Finally, we arrived in China. I took a deep breath, collected my items, and deplaned. All passengers had to go through customs and immigration. As I stood in line, I prayed, "Lord, give me favor in the eyes of the officials." The next moment I was waved over to an immigration booth. The moment of decision had arrived.

As I stood before the agent – a very businesslike middle-aged woman – she asked for my passport. She scrutinized it along with my other documents, looked up and studied my face for a moment, and returned my documents. Without hesitation, she reached over and grabbed her hand-stamp and stamped my passport. I thanked her as she signaled the next person in line. Oh, what joy!

Once I left the airport, I made one stop, and from there

my sister and I planned to visit my mom's final resting place. I wanted to pay my respects, and the cemetery was only five minutes away. As we walked together, I asked about mom's last minutes. "What did she say? What were her thoughts?"

My sister related what took place during our mom's last moments, before going to be with the Lord. She said, "Mom knew her time to depart had come. She told me there was no time for Sarah to visit now, and to tell Sarah that it's okay. 'If I don't see her here on earth, I will see her in heaven.'" My mom also left another message for me with my sister. She said, "Tell Sarah, the most important thing in her life is to continue to follow Jesus." And with other words, she spoke her heart and surrendered her spirit to the Lord.

I asked my sister about the funeral service. She said, "Mom made a special request that she be given a Christian service, and she vehemently rejected the Chinese cultural death rites." These rites included things like burning incense and paper to appease the spirits. Mom wanted nothing to do with that superstition, but in my hometown, cremation of the deceased on the day of their death was the custom. In order to fulfill my mom's wishes, my youngest brother hurried to the church and spoke with the leaders to come and conduct a proper Christian funeral service.

Everything was so last-minute and rushed that the leaders hesitated. My brother passionately begged them to honor Mom's request. He even offered them money to come and fulfill Mom's dying request. They rejected the money and came to serve the family in this last request. Everyone was grateful for the service provided for my mom, and my family members prepared food for all in attendance. During this time, they continually expressed gratitude for the service, and no one in my family insisted on Chinese cultural traditions. They were all committed to honor all Mom wanted.

Once we reached the cemetery, a flood of emotions filled my every fiber as I approached Mom's grave. On the one hand, I was genuinely happy she was in the presence of the Lord. On the other hand, I was sad that I didn't get to say and do all the things I had in my heart to express to Mom. Now, I stood before her grave.

It had been four years since Mom passed away. Overwhelming grief had enveloped me the moment I heard of her passing. I couldn't be comforted. When my husband returned home, he saw my distress and asked, "What happened?" Panic filled his face. At first, I couldn't even answer him. I cried like a baby with no comfort in sight. Finally, I replied through sobs and tears. "My . . . my mom isn't . . . isn't alive anymore." To this day, he says he's never seen me so distraught. Even my Romero family tried to comfort me, as did many other friends, but no words or kind gestures could relieve my grief. I simply couldn't stop crying.

Part of my sorrow was due to the guilt I felt for not doing more for Mom. How I would have liked to lift a cup of refreshing water to her lips to ease her pain. But she was in China, and I was in the U.S. The distance between us devoured me.

My only comfort came from the Spirit who helped me to pray. "Heavenly Father, thank you for giving me such a great mom. She is with you now, and for that I am happy, but I miss her terribly."

Now, standing in front of her grave, I saw her picture etched on the stone. I bowed down and gently kissed the picture and said my official good-bye. My mourning and joy were now complete. I stood and walked away from her gravesite and walked home arm in arm with my sister. Mom was in the hands of the Good Shepherd.

Reuniting with My Father

Once, during a phone visit, my father reminded me, "You said you would come back and visit me. So, when will you come? I am old; there is no more time to wait." His request was so pure. His words pierced my heart. He was right. I needed to figure out how to fulfill my promise.

I called on all my friends and church family to pray that God would keep my father alive so I'd be able to see him again. But most importantly, so I'd be able to share the gospel with him again. Whatever the risks might be, I thought them well worth it. I was willing to pay the price to accomplish this visit, again.

Now, my sister, nieces, and I stood before my father. He looked at each of us, then said, "Welcome home Xianxiu, Lili, and Pingping." He looked at me confused, then pointed his finger at me and asked, "Who is she?"

My elderly father was almost completely deaf, so my sister Xianxiu drew close to him and shouted, "She is Sarah! She has come back to visit you as she promised!"

Surprise and wonder washed across his face. "Sarah? It is Sarah?" Tears filled his eyes. He turned to me and in a quivering voice said, "Finally, I see you. You are home."

Tears spilled down my cheeks as his words penetrated my heart in a way I didn't anticipate. This moment was like no other. God granted me a holy moment with my daddy. I approached him slowly and hugged him tightly with all my love and longing. I could feel his overflowing heart of love and happiness. Even these words fail to capture this holy moment when joy flooded my soul.

My hometown seemed foreign to me, but my daddy's heart and my sisters and brothers showered me with love and acceptance. In fact, for the next twenty days, they competed with one another for my attention. I felt so honored with celebration after celebration, feast upon feast; the festivities were nonstop. The constant theme was "Sarah is home. Yes, little sister is with us again."

My father asked many questions about America. "What do you do in America? Are you happy in America? Does your husband treat you well?" Then he pressed me and asked, "Can you come back once a year?" He went on to say that he saw a foreign movie that showed Americans hugging each other when they meet. "Does that really happen?" I saddled up really close to him and took him by surprise as I hugged and kissed his face over and over again. He laughed so heartily that the whole family joined in a chorus of laughter.

One evening, while at my third brother's house having a celebration, my daddy didn't see me come in. He asked, "Where is the guest of honor? Where is Sarah?" I quietly walked up behind him, taking advantage of his deafness, and turned quickly to him and smothered him with kisses, saying, "Here I am." His wit never skipped a beat. He said, "Come home with me. I don't ever want to lose you again."

Every day, I wrote letters of love to him. He'd read these letters and keep them close to his heart. At age ninety-five, the only physical issue my daddy struggled with was near-deafness. I was so grateful to God for the grace He had shown to my daddy's physical well-being. On one occasion, I wrote a note to my dad, which said, "Daddy, I want you to believe in Jesus, then you can see Mama again!"

He said, "I believe in God. Your mama regularly attended church, now I regret that I did not. I am old and it is difficult to get around."

I continued praying for my daddy, as I sought open doors of ministry to him and my family. Being in my beloved China again, and visiting my daddy and family was good for me. Visiting my mom's gravesite and holding tightly to my father reminded me of how much love and pride I have in my parents. My heart's desire is to be their crown of joy both now and for all eternity.

WHAT DO YOU THINK?

How is or was your relationship with your parents? For some, this will be a delightful question, and for others, a regretful reminder. If you've read my previous books, you know my standing with my parents wasn't what it is now. God made a way for me; I trust He will make a way for you too.

TODAY'S REFLECTION

_____
_____
_____
_____
_____
_____
_____
_____
_____
_____
_____
_____
_____

TODAY'S PRAYER

_____
_____
_____
_____
_____
_____

DAY 30

God's Victory, My Blessing

Then he threw his arms around his brother
Benjamin and wept, and Benjamin embraced him,
weeping. And he kissed all his brothers and wept
over them. Afterward his brothers talked with him.
(Genesis 45:14-15)

Here's the backstory:

Book II: Day 1

The next day, I walked all the way home while rejoicing and singing songs to the Lord. I had no idea what was about to happen. As I approached my home, from afar, I saw my father and brothers at the gate. As I got closer, I saw anger in their faces, but I wasn't alarmed.

Once inside, my father insisted I sit in a chair. I sat, not realizing the chair was to be used to question me. Anger seethed in his voice as he asked, "Where have you been these last three days?"

"I have come to believe in Jesus," I said.

At that moment, my father, with my brothers' consent, slapped me across the face with such force that I flew from the chair and hit the floor. This response to the beautiful thing God had done was so unexpected.

Book II: Preface

My father and brothers provided fierce opposition to my mother and me. As a result of us becoming followers of Jesus, my father gave us an ultimatum: "Your Jesus or me!" We chose Jesus and were forced out of our house. In anger, my father and brothers gathered all our belongings and pajamas and tossed them out of the house onto the street. The two of us slowly regained our composure and carefully picked up our belongings on that cold winter day.

I looked at my mom. "What do we do now?"

"Even if we have to beg," she said, "we will still believe in Jesus. Let's gather everything and go."

And later in my story:

Book II: Day 20

That night, they held a family intervention with the goal of getting me to stay with the family and not go the way of harm and prison again. After they all pleaded their case, they saw that, although moved emotionally, I was determined to rejoin my church family. Their disappointment turned to anger, which they directed at my mom.

"If only you didn't make her go to church with you!" they shouted at her. "See what you have done? You've ruined her young life. What will become of her?"

My mom defended herself by asserting that the decisions I had made, I made of my own free will. But their anger wasn't appeased. At one point, my father shoved her and said, "You, an old woman, have destroyed Sarah's young life."

I assured my family that it was not Mom's fault. What she had done for me by bringing me to Christ was the greatest gift. In my heart of hearts, the ministry Jesus called me to was unfinished. I had to return to the gospel field immediately.

As you can see, this was no mere falling out with my family because of religious faith. This was open hostility toward my mother and me for following Christ. If I rated this on a scale with a +10 saying yes to Christ and a "0" as total indifference, my father and brothers were at a -10. To them, Christ was the worst thing that could possibly happen to me. This gives you the context to my story as I returned to China. This is where this chapter begins . . . but doesn't end.

My sister and two nephews picked me up from the airport. We visited for a week and then boarded a high-speed rail for my hometown. This was just under a five-hour trip. How my China has changed, I thought. A high-speed rail.

I arrived in my hometown about 4:00 p.m. and was rushed to meet with my daddy. From there, I was escorted to a restaurant specially reserved for my welcome-home party. No sooner did we walk in than I saw my brothers and their families. Everyone was there.

My brothers said, "Welcome home, mei mei!" and embraced me with sincere happiness and tears of joy. I went around the room and hugged all my brothers and then everyone else. As you can imagine, it was an emotional time, especially in light of the open animosity a decade earlier.

This is like a dream, I thought, but it's real. While on the flight to China, I tried to recall my life in China and to remember their faces. Now they stood before me and I was so overwhelmed by the moment that I was speechless.

At the table, we began to speak. Slowly at first, but then questions and answers bounced back and forth, rapidly overlapping and colliding as we talked over one another. Yes, it was very chaotic, but extremely enjoyable, just looking around at all their faces, their gestures, and manners. "This is my family!" I cried out in my heart. I was pleased that I was so loved, especially as I reflected on our last time together before I departed back to the gospel field. Now, we were at peace. It was as though our hearts had grown fonder. Forgiveness and love flowed throughout our gathering. Truly, grace and joy were experienced by young and old alike. Where did the -10 hostility go? Did the Lord use Mom to soften their hearts? Or did the Lord use others to help my family draw closer to Him?

During that gathering, we worked out a schedule that allowed each sibling to entertain me in their home. The days ahead were full of family time and dining.

Not many days later, I was treated to another gathering that included my fourth brother and all my siblings. What fun! Food and family make a wonderful combination, then add to that kara-oke, and all family inhibitions evaporated. It was such pure fun, singing with my brothers and dancing together – great family time. I was catching up on all the lost time with my family. The night culminated with all of us joining in karaoke, singing arm in arm, with tears streaming down our faces. But something more than singing was happening, and we all knew it. Thank you, Lord, for my family.

Besides fun times and catching up, something bigger was happening. The Lord showed me that my family was softening to Him. When we visited my second brother's grave, they were mindful to excuse me from their traditional anniversary rites. How thoughtful. In fact, they insisted that I not indulge with them. I knew this wasn't to exclude me, but out of respect for me and my devotion to Christ.

On another occasion, my third sister-in-law, who was led to the Lord by my mom, clearly shared my mom's boldness and determination without family rejection.

Lastly, my first brother and his wife invited me over to their home, and we talked deeply about God. Then, I asked them to pray with me.

"But I don't know how to pray," my brother said, and his wife nodded in agreement.

"We've never prayed before," she said.

I said, "Let me pray aloud for you both." They happily agreed. No sooner did I say "Amen" than my brother began praying openly. I was amazed. Remember, they were a -10. Now he openly prayed to my God. No sooner did he finish saying his "Amen" than his wife took up praying to Jesus unashamedly. After all was done, I rejoiced, saying, "Lord Jesus, this is beyond all my expectations. Thank you for Your great grace!"

Saying Farewell

Time spent with my family passed with lightning speed. Before I knew it, the time had come to say good-bye. As I prepared to say farewell, I reflectively looked out the window of my room. Raindrops gently fell outside, and in my heart an emotional storm brewed. I was trying to be strong.

During my stay, I had the privilege of caring physically for my daddy. Like an emotional sponge, I absorbed every moment with him. I fussed over him by buying him fresh clean linens and blankets so he would be warm on these winter nights. I inspected his clothes to make sure he would be well dressed in the days ahead. I went through his pantry, double checked his food supply and its nutritional value, and made sure he had a bountiful food supply.

The week before, I made it a point to share every meal with him. I served up hot food on our cold mornings and evenings as we sat wearing our big coats. Our hot bowls warmed our hands and satisfied our hunger. As we quietly sat sharing a meal, I could see happiness on his face – I think he knew I loved being his little girl again. I know I did. I wanted to do all in my power to make him happy. I tried to make up for the time lost as father and daughter, but the time was overshadowed by the knowledge that I would be leaving again. I wrote a note to him, because with his hearing problem, I wanted to be sure he understood. It said, "Daddy, I will be leaving on Monday, December twenty-sixth."

As he read the note, his countenance changed. He looked like a sad child. He raised his hand and slowly counted, "Twenty-two, twenty-three, twenty-four, twenty-five, and twenty-six; there are only five days left!" I nodded. He asked, "Can you stay for Chinese New Year?" His request was simple and as pure as the fresh-driven snow. I studied his ninety-five-year-old face and my pent-up emotions poured forth like the storm I anticipated. Tears brimmed to overflowing and ran down my cheeks. I turned my face away, unsuccessfully trying to hide my heart laid bare.

He said, "If your mom was still alive, I would not be so lonely. Can you visit me every year?"

I wrote out, "I will think about it."

He said, "You live so far away from me that coming home to me will be very difficult." Then he bargained with me. "How about coming back to visit me every other year?" Then, in all sincerity, he said, "Perhaps there won't be a next time." We both knew of his advanced age and understood the possibility of his death. Then he changed the focus. He pressed me and wanted me to make a promise. "You and your husband should make it a point to visit your sister and brothers and all your nieces and nephews." I slowly nodded. It devastated me to see tears stream down his face. I cried to the Lord, "Abba Father, what can I say at a time like this?"

My adult nieces wrote to me: "Auntie, we were so disappointed that we couldn't sleep with you during your visit. Now you're leaving us. We can't sleep, we only cry at night while our families sleep. Let us sleep with you before you leave. We want you to hold us while we sleep, like when we were babies . . . do you remember? We were all so little when you left home."

One particular adult niece said, "I visited you while you were in prison, do you remember? Because of the circumstances, I had you in my life for only a little while. Now I'm grown up and have my own family. My sons who never met you before are more attached to you in this short time than they are to me, their mother!"

I can still hear the sweet sounds of my grandnephews' voices: "Enpo! [gracious grandmother] Let's play another game. We love you so much!" I held their precious little hands and kissed their handsome faces. I drank in every moment with them, and chased them around and around the house. This newfound attachment to these little handsome boys made my departure more painful, but it was a pain I gladly bore to have them close to me.

As I prepared to leave, my sister openly sobbed, as if we'd never see each other again. In these wonderfully painful and awkward final moments, I stepped forward to embrace my brother and eventually, every member of my family. We lingered in each other's arms; only our tears told the unspoken story of our renewed love for each other. "Abba Father," I prayed as I drove away. "Now let my pent-up heart break forth like a flood." And as we pulled away, it did.

I waved to them as they stood watching me, angling to get the last glimpse. Their forms became smaller and smaller, but our love for each other grew bigger than life itself. At that moment, in an utterance of praise, I said, "God, You resurrected the relationship between my family and me. Twenty years of separation and distance, from China to America and back, yet it was as if no time – no distance – was too great for You. I am convinced in my heart, Lord, that You are preparing them for Your great salvation. They have come such a long way. I know You will not fail them. Yes, You are the victorious God, You are the God of Joseph who served You and You blessed his family, especially his father, Jacob."

WHAT DO YOU THINK?

Who is the most hostile to you because of your faith? Does it seem impossible for them ever to turn to the Lord? I had committed my family to Christ, but to see God at work in them was amazing. Can Jesus do that for you? Why not pray anew for that hostile person and let's see what God will do?

TODAY'S REFLECTION

_____

_____

_____

_____

_____

_____

_____

_____

_____

_____

_____

_____

TODAY'S PRAYER

_____

_____

_____

_____

_____

Acknowledgements: *Bob Fu, China Aid; The Golf Course Road Church of Christ; Mid-Cities Church; Uncle Doug and Auntie Angie; Matthew Rose of Voice of the Martyrs; the Romero family; Bill Welsh of Refuge Calvary Chapel, Huntington Beach; Hacienda Christian Fellowship, La Puente; and my husband, Joshua, who quietly supported me in all my work along with many other supporters.*

Meet the Author

After her conversion, Sarah Liu (pictured above with her father) became a traveling evangelist to the villages of South China; she was arrested three times and served in the notorious Laojiao labor camps. Following her release, she was sent by her house church to the US to be a voice for the persecuted Christians in China.

For information about volumes 1 and 2 of Sarah Liu's *Journey of Faith* series, see the following pages.

Life abounds with crises, disappointments, mundane routines, and some very joyful moments. Everything that happens has a cause. We often don't take time to reflect on purposes, or we simply explain events away with simplistic explanations of either good or bad luck. Totally unaware of real causes behind life events, we easily move on to the next day, the next week, and the next year. In a gentle way, Sarah Liu leads the reader on a walk through events from her childhood in China and shows the handprint of God on these vignettes of her life. As she reflects on what God accomplished through joys, crises, disappointments, and ordinary family life, she invites readers to reflect on their own life experiences to detect the hand of God. Her conviction that God selects and covers with grace regardless of man's perceptions runs throughout her stories and provides encouragement and inspiring faith and trust. This book provides encouragement for anyone praying for a loved one to come to God, but also provides rich inspiration for those with pressing questions about the meaning and purpose of life's crises and disappointments. Parents, pastors, ministers, teachers, and leaders would be inspired by this devotional written from a genuine passion to explore God's present action in life's daily events.

Available where books are sold.

"Best story to enrich your life ... Sarah Liu's story is the most appealing illustration of sufferology."
  -Dr. Bob Fu, founder/president of China Aid Association and author of God's Double Agent

"When Sarah Liu gave her heart to the Lord, she decided to follow Him no matter what the cost-and in her case the cost was great. What we have in this book is a gripping narrative, accompanied by some probing questions about our own personal Christian walk. If you want to learn about persecution in China and at the same time how to live a victorious life in Christ, then this is the book for you. But it does come with a health warning-be prepared to be challenged."
  -Mervyn Thomas, chief executive, Christian Solidarity Worldwide, London, United Kingdom

"Sarah Liu is a spiritual giant. For years, she endured unspeakable torture and did not break, despite the combined forces of evil of the Chinese Communist Party. This is a book for today, as the persecution of Christians is on the rise the world over, and in the United States as well."
  -Reggie Littlejohn, founder/president, Women's Rights Without Frontiers; graduate of Yale Law School

Available where books are sold.

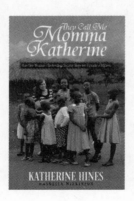

Do you ever sell yourself short? That's what Katherine Hines did before she realized she was selling God short. After years of tragedies, Katherine learned that God could do more in her life than she ever imagined if she trusted Him and believed. She discovered that He wants to change lives through us and bless us in the process. Whoever we are, wherever we came from, God can use us to make a difference in someone's life.

Katherine's story begins with tragedies, but God touched her heart at a crusade and led her to Uganda as a missionary to the children. Leaving her prestigious job and home, she went to a land of mud huts and polluted water. In the midst of sickness and poverty, she loved and cared for the orphans of the war-torn country, as she faced witch doctors and Muslim agitators. Katherine shares her life story to help us know that we can all make a difference – if only we let God. . . .

Available where books are sold.

American bush pilot Russell Stendal, on routine business, landed his plane in a remote Colombian village. Gunfire exploded throughout the town and within minutes Russell's 142-day ordeal had begun. The Colombian cartel explained that this was a kidnapping for ransom and that he would be held until payment was made.

Held at gunpoint deep in the jungle and with little else to occupy his time, Russell got ahold of some paper and began to write. He told the story of his life and kept a record of his experience in the guerrilla camp. His "book" became a bridge to the men who held him hostage and now serves as the basis for this incredible true story of how God's love penetrated a physical and ideological jungle.

Available where books are sold.